Confidence at Work
Get it, feel it, keep it

Confidence at Work
Get it, feel it, keep it

ROS TAYLOR

KoganPage

LONDON PHILADELPHIA NEW DELHI

First published in Great Britain and the United States in 2011 by Kogan Page Limited

120 Pentonville Road	1518 Walnut Street, Suite 1100	4737/23 Ansari Road
London N1 9JN	Philadelphia PA 19102	Daryaganj
United Kingdom	USA	New Delhi 110002
www.koganpage.com		India

© Ros Taylor, 2011

The right of Ros Taylor to be identified as the author of this work has been asserted by her in accordance with the Copyright, Designs and Patents Act 1988.

ISBN   978 0 7494 6121 8
E-ISBN 978 0 7494 6122 5

British Library Cataloguing-in-Publication Data

A CIP record for this book is available from the British Library.

Library of Congress Cataloging-in-Publication Data

Taylor, Ros.
  Confidence at work : get it, feel it, keep it / Ros Taylor.
    p. cm.
  Includes bibliographical references.
  ISBN 978-0-7494-6121-8 – ISBN 978-0-7494-6122-5   1. Self-confidence.
2. Success.   3. Success in business.   4. Work–Psychological aspects.
I. Title.
  BF575.S39T384 2011
  158.7–dc22

                     2010033136

Typeset by Graphicraft Ltd, Hong Kong
Production managed by Jellyfish
Printed in the UK by CPI Antony Rowe

Contents

To my husband John Young

Before we start

Dear Reader,

Learning is about stories and to learn about confidence I would love to hear about yours.

I am interested in your journey towards confidence at work. Was there a turning point, a theory that provided understanding, an experience that helped you to believe in yourself, a course that provided you with the skills for confidence? Let me hear about it in order to share your experience with others. Stories inspire and provide hope for change and success.

You may also have some tips for confidence at work, some challenge that you have overcome and emerged a more confident person as a result.

Write to me on my blog at **www.rostaylorgroup.com** I will respond and so will others with their experiences.

I too am still on my journey towards confidence at work as life is always throwing up challenges. So we can gain more confidence together.

Happy reading and I hope to hear from you soon.

Best wishes,
Ros

Confidence starts here

If there were ever a time when confidence was needed at work it is now. In a post-subprime mortgage society with a more challenging marketplace, fewer jobs and more people after them, the skills associated with confidence have never been of more use. My work with executives has also made me realize that there is a higher level of confidence necessary to be successful and to be a leader of a team, department or company in today's world.

Having lived a little, I realize that confidence is a journey. It is not a series of quick fixes with a finite end; it is a continuous state of mind and a lifetime's work. I decided to ask a wide variety of people I met over the period of a month to tell me about their journeys towards confidence so that I could relay them to you in this book, *Confidence at Work*.

I also had to change from being a shy, only child who always wanted to be someone else to being the much happier me I am today. As an individual, I have sought out theories and skills for confidence to help myself, but then as a psychologist, have passed these concepts on to my clients. Let's face it, if it worked for me then surely this approach could work for you.

So that's what this book is about: how to achieve a high level of confidence to go for promotion and become the sort of leader others have the confidence to follow. This is also about my journey towards self-confidence – the insights and theories I have discovered so that you can embark on your own journey as a result.

I was at the graduation ceremony of a group of senior scientists who had just completed my Leadership Programme. As a finale they had to give a presentation in front of an invited audience of company vice-presidents (VPs) about what they had learned. Without exception they were reflective, informed and funny, with wonderful examples of how their new skills had transformed their leadership style and their lives. It had been a year's programme with personal profiling, in-depth exploration of the meaning of leadership in corporate life as well as skills input to inspire others around them to lead. We laughed, we cried, we were awed by the changes they had wrought in their lives and we were impressed as much by the quality of delivery as the content of what was presented. When I asked those invited VPs for feedback, they all mentioned one word – confidence. I was nonplussed. I expected more comments about behaviour change, return on investment or something at least more specific. Not just 'confidence'.

It reminded me of the time when I interviewed 80 chief executives for my book *Fast Track to the Top*. After personal profiling, the completion of checklists of skills that took them to the top and an open-ended interview which explored their rise to seniority and success, I asked in summary what had made them successful. Too often to be coincidental they replied that they had been 'lucky'. After all their struggles, experiences and learning they thought they were lucky?

I have spent my life as a psychologist believing that you create your own destiny and now these high fliers were ascribing their ascendancy to luck! Of course I didn't mention my irritation at the time, but I had cause to reflect on what they said over the years. I came eventually to the conclusion that they had, as the result of a successful life, felt blessed and, yes, lucky. Luck is, I think, a positive state of mind that not only helps people become successful but is also an outcome of that success.

I remember interviewing a senior executive at *Reader's Digest* for a BBC radio programme on social science research. He divulged that when readers won even a small amount of money this changed their thinking about themselves quite dramatically. They became winners rather than losers and started to talk about themselves as lucky.

Happiness is also of this ilk. You really have to do things to achieve a happiness outcome. The bluebird of happiness does not just alight on your shoulder and, hey presto, you are happy. You have to look at relationships, finances, work, and a meaningful existence to get to that state of bliss.

So I suppose confidence is just the same. Like luck and happiness, confidence is the outcome of a whole lot of stuff: thinking style, emotional well-being, experience, opportunity, prescience, personality, leadership, decision making, problem solving and pure skill. There is always room for more confidence.

The people I talked to about confidence are listed below and their comments are scattered throughout the book. This was not a tight piece of research under strictly controlled conditions but more a series of interesting encounters that I ruthlessly exploited on your behalf. There were young entrepreneurs, corporate CEOs, head-hunters, charity leaders and thought leaders like Tony Buzan and Daniel Goleman. All had views of a differing nature about confidence: its definition, how it revealed itself at work and where they were on the confidence continuum.

I asked them what they looked for in addition to expertise when recruiting staff, so that I could relay the results to you in Chapter 8. I was interested in what immediately struck them in a candidate so that you could attain the confidence and skills to sparkle in the same way.

My list of 20 participants

Tony Buzan – Inventor of Mind Mapping™

Andi Keeling – Head of Learning for the Royal Bank of Scotland

Geraldine Gammell – Director of the Prince's Trust

Ian McMillan – Director of CBI Scotland

Peter Lederer – Chairman of Gleneagles Hotels

Daniel Goleman – Author of *Emotional Intelligence*

Tom DiPuma – Global Sales Leader

Brian Lang – Executive Coach and former Vice Chancellor of St Andrews University

Oli Norman – Founder of DADA PR

Selma Hunter – Vice President of the Process Division, Jacobs Engineering

Rosalyn Rahme – Recruitment Consultant with Goldjobs

Angela Middleton – Recruitment Consultant with Middleton Murray

George Morris – MD Morris Spottiswood

Philip Rodney – Chairman of Burness Solicitors

Professor Susan Hart – Dean of Strathclyde University Business School

Fraser Doherty – Founder and MD of SuperJam

John Young – Environmentalist

Rob MacLachlan – Editor of *People Management*

Tari Lang – Executive Coach and Reputation Management Expert

Alan Macdonald – MD Dawn Group & Ayr Race Course

You can see the short questionnaire I used below and sadly some didn't complete it, as they rushed on stage and spoke to an audience of hundreds or left to attend a board meeting. Some I met at dinners, so I had to remember the questions and write the answers on the backs of menus. I felt it was not the done thing to whip the checklist out of my handbag! So I apologize for any sense of things being unplanned but the responses were worth acquiring.

Complete the Confidence questionnaire and Self-esteem checklist yourself:

Confidence questionnaire

How does confidence show itself to you in others:
  a at first meeting?
  b in someone's thinking?
  c in their emotions?
  d in their behaviour?	

If recruiting staff to your team or business what do you look for in addition to specific expertise?	
How confident are you when interviewed yourself?	
When did you first find your voice to speak up and what was the situation?	
When are you most confident?	
When are you least confident?	
What areas of confidence might you still have to work on?	
If you increased your confidence even more right now what could you achieve?	

Many of the replies to the Confidence questionnaire are scattered throughout the book.

Highlights

There were some highlights. Brian Lang thought that if his wife Tari were any more confident she would be dangerous.

I loved Tom DiPuma's input that confidence was knowing the words to the song. I liked it so much as a symbol for articulating who you are and what you do, I used it as a heading. And of course meeting Tony Buzan and getting his input was wonderful. He felt that confidence was 'self joy' and also a belief that whatever situations life throws at you, you will find a solution. He described himself as an intellectual delinquent when he discovered that the school system only rewarded a certain kind of intelligence. His pal was brilliant at spotting birds and understanding nature, but since there was no exam for that he was bottom of the class. Tony was determined to find another way. And Mind Mapping™ certainly helped the majority of us to pass exams, construct business plans and write books!

Finally, Daniel Goleman's comment about bad confidence being 'a narcissistic over-inflation of capabilities' was glorious. It so describes the struttingly arrogant. I asked, at the end of our interview, when he had found his voice to speak up about his beliefs and he replied that it was early on at school. He hoped that it was with a realistic sense of capability but, he mused in retrospect, perhaps not.

Self-esteem checklist

Tick where you agree with the statement:

1	I understand my strengths	
2	I know intuitively what is right for me	
3	I am sincere	
4	I fear nothing	
5	I have challenged all of the beliefs that were holding me back	
6	I have high self-esteem	
7	I do not judge myself	
8	Life feels effortless now	
9	I do only what I value	
10	I never tell others what to do	
11	I am never intolerant	
12	I hate nothing	
13	I like myself	
14	I am aware of my life's purpose	
15	My thoughts are positive	
16	I never belittle others	
17	I compete with no one	
18	I inspire others	
19	Life is a joy	
20	I am worthy of all I receive	
21	I allow others to be confident and shine	

Self-esteem checklist results

Results taken from 14 out of 20 interviewees. Recorded in order of most agreed statement.

I understand my strengths	14
I inspire others	13
I know intuitively what is right for me	12
I like myself	12
My thoughts are positive	12
Life is a joy	11
I am sincere	11
I never belittle others	10
I am aware of my life's purpose	8
I have high self-esteem	8
I am worthy of all I receive	8
I allow others to be confident and shine	7
I do only what I value	7
I do not judge myself	5
I hate nothing	5
I compete with no one	3
I never tell others what to do	2
I have challenged all of the beliefs that were holding me back	2
Life feels effortless now	2
I fear nothing	1
I am never intolerant	1

The self-esteem statements which received only five ratings or less could be described as the areas of development for this group of senior and successful people. Many mentioned that they did still judge themselves and found themselves wanting on occasion. Some also commented that they thought that competition was good, if not the destructive kind, which seemed fair to me. They disliked the current trend in education that allowed for no winners or losers. Life is competitive and the sooner children and adults handle the results of that the better, they said.

Very few felt that life was effortless and thought that they would have to be meditative yogis to be in that state of bliss in today's business climate. Many told me that they struggled with not telling people what to do and being completely tolerant. They realized that a coaching approach was the one of choice, but when up against it they could resort to command and control. This is definitely an area for development for this group.

As for fearing nothing, they confided that there is much to fear out there in the business world at the moment and they struggle with that daily. Perhaps with confidence that fear can be reduced.

When I looked at individual scores on the Self-esteem checklist, all 14 completers achieved above-average scores for self-esteem. Top of the list, however, was Tony Buzan, Mr Mind Mapping™, with 17 out of a possible 21 ticks in boxes, closely followed by Rob MacLachlan, editor of *People Management*, with 16. Clearly they practise what they preach.

Add up the scores on your own checklist. Those areas you didn't tick are your goals for confidence. When you complete the book add some actions around these areas so that you can increase your confidence in life and work.

Figures 4.1, 5.1, 9.1, 9.2, 11.2, 19.1 and 19.2 are available as downloadable Word documents on the Kogan Page website.

To access, go to www.koganpage.com/ConfidenceAtWork and enter the password: CAW4866

Part One
Who are you anyway...?

Chapter One
Bring yourself
to work

Who are you anyway and what can you bring to the world of work? We are all so busy living inside our heads that it is difficult to objectify our distinct contribution. However this discovery is essential to increasing your confidence at work. Many of the people who discussed the nature of confidence with me mentioned self-awareness as being at the very heart of confidence at work.

Daniel Goleman, of Emotional Intelligence fame, spoke to me on a recent visit to London about his views. He felt there were two sides to confidence. In his words: 'Healthy confidence is a high sense of self-awareness with a true understanding of what you are good at. Bad confidence is a narcissistic over-inflation of capabilities.' For me that sounds more like arrogance than confidence. But let's not get too precious about semantics.

Selma Hunter, VP of the Process Division, Jacobs Engineering, says: 'My definition of confidence is an understanding of what my strengths and weaknesses are and leveraging these strengths without being arrogant.' Selma is a woman in the male-dominated engineering profession. She not only started the Process Division but exceeded expected first-year profits by a multiple of four. She was of course promoted to vice president.

Former Vice Chancellor of St Andrews University, Brian Lang, felt that: 'Confidence at work is an awareness of your ability to deliver.' Brian knows all about delivery as he headed up the British Library project delivering on one of the most exciting new 'fit for purpose buildings' in London.

Working strengths

So these replies led me to reflect on when I knew what my working strengths and ability to deliver were. As an only child born of loving middle-class parents, I hadn't a clue who I was, never mind what I could contribute. Position in a larger family gives you some definition of where you fit in and the role you play. I was free form, with no boundaries but also with no sibling feedback. So it was as if I grew up in a vacuum. I did know, however, that I liked to talk a lot and sing but found it difficult to stand from a cross-legged position on the floor, which provided great angst at gym class. These aspects of me have persisted to this day. However, with a career in psychology I can talk and sing if I feel so inclined and I don't have to get up from the floor with my legs crossed. Done deal.

I am convinced this lack of personal awareness drove me to read psychology at university. I had always wanted to go on to higher education but, in retrospect, for all the wrong reasons. I used to go past Glasgow University on the 10A bus with my mother. There was a cafe called 'the Papingo' on the corner, which served frothy coffee, as it was called in those days, with interestingly skinny, black-attired students lounging louchely outside discussing, I presumed, the esoteric niceties of philosophy or politics. It all looked so debauched and glorious. Of course, by the time I matriculated, the cafe had closed and I would never know if these 'über cool' students had been debating existentialism or eyeing up talent. Probably the latter.

I was hungry for intellectual stimulation and of course for a bit of personal debauchery too, but with no idea what I was eventually going to do with all this learning. I did not get around to deciding that psychology was my academic choice till the second year and then it was Saul on the road to Damascus. I simply loved it. My journey with psychology and confidence was always driven by trying to understand myself and then subsequently my clients. This upfront analysis of how the bits of a person fit together is, I discovered later on, much underestimated and underutilized by psychologists and coaches alike. However, this investigation to me defines psychological intervention. It is a kind of 'House' of the mind; a cross between Hugh Laurie, Columbo and Sherlock Holmes.

The glorious thing about *Homo sapiens* is that everything we think, feel and do is an extension of what is truly 'us'; a bit like a radio mast with waves spinning around it. This radial nature of who we are permits the exploration of all sorts of personal aspects using theories of psychology, psychometric tests, personality profiles and other more symbolic exercises. All reveal different pieces of what makes us unique.

The theories and practice of psychology I uncovered on my journey for enlightenment I will share with you throughout this book and, where I can, I will adapt questionnaires and checklists so you can share in these insights. And of course the more you know about yourself and what you offer, the more you will enjoy your own journey with confidence.

Nature versus nurture

At a basic level during my degree course I was beginning to understand that a strength I had was an interest in people and what made them tick. The nature versus nurture debate was in full swing when I was studying and was tipping towards nurture as the major influence in our lives rather than genetics. It was such a hopeful time, the 60s and 70s. So I shouldn't have found it surprising that with a mother who talked to anything that moved I might be so disposed myself. I took her on the tour of Buckingham Palace, which takes normal people two hours to navigate all the rooms. Five hours later, having talked to every member of staff and uniformed flunky, we emerged blinking into the dusk. Of course they loved someone being so interested.

Once, after visiting Wimbledon in the former standing room only section, my mother found herself in the Royal toilet and chatted about the match even-handedly between Princesses Margaret and Alexandra as they washed their hands. Clearly used to such interactions, she forgot to tell me till we were travelling home.

My mother is also very assertive. She knew what she wanted and single-mindedly went after it. Not for her a restaurant table outside the toilet. To this day we often move three or four times till we achieve the right seat, usually by the window. She also liked a green banana. If the poor banana became prematurely yellow or dared sport a brown spot, back it went. I used to cower with embarrassment behind the vegetables as she returned the offending item. I there and then vowed never to be like my mother. Yesterday, a London bus accelerated past me on a zebra crossing missing me by centimetres. Before I could say 'green bananas' I was knocking at the driver's window calmly telling him that what he had just done was against the law and the pursuit of Grand Prix status in his bus would be at the expense of his licence. I had officially become my mother.

Reflections of childhood

It is worth carrying out your own reflections of childhood, as they can reveal what you are truly like and what you love to do. But what has this to do with work? Being in touch with who you are, where you have come from, your family background and childhood aspirations help define your contribution at work. If you choose a job that you might be able to do but does not tap into your major strengths, then you will be eternally frustrated. Never feel that 'it is just a job' so any one will do. Work can be fulfilling and challenging, stretching capabilities way beyond your wildest dreams. This is the stuff of confidence.

The more you bring yourself to work, the more unique will be your contribution and the swifter will be your path to success. Compliant conscripts at work tend to be ignored when promotions are handed out whereas vociferous volunteers are heard and fostered.

In the next chapters I want to share with you my favourite theories in psychology so that you will be better able to understand yourself and as a result become more confident at work.

Steps to confidence at work

- Begin to understand your working strengths by looking back to childhood, as that is when they emerged.

- Look at your parents and see where you might have inherited or learned your skills.

- Reflect back on childhood aspirations and calculate whether you are still on track to fulfil these or have chosen different ones to pursue. Are these the correct ones to satisfy your desire for confidence and success? If not, readjust your goals.

- Don't settle, seek success.

Chapter Two
Eric Berne's transactional analysis

Eric Berne, in the late 1950s, suggested that we are like our parents not perhaps in the content of our lives but in the way we communicate. His theory of transactional analysis is based on the belief that we can learn from studying more closely the way our decisions and communications are based on our thoughts and feelings. He proposed the concept that all experiences were laid down on a 'tape' during our early years to be accessed later when necessary. Although we can't remember the first three years of our lives that tape was even then recording and is still playing back to this day. Berne has it that there are three aspects to our behaviour – the parent, the child and the adult. He calls these aspects 'egos'.

The parent ego

The parent ego has two sides: the critical, disciplining, restricting parent and the helpful, caring, loving parent. The controlling parent is the one who scolds when the children are late for dinner and the caring parent is the one who is happy they arrived home safely.

In Berne's theory, our parents were a huge influence in our lives. The basic information that we use comes from a lifetime of experience with our parents and teachers, particularly in early life. Remarks such as 'Sit up straight at the table', 'Use your knife and fork not your fingers', 'Bring it here, mummy will help you', will be on your parent tape whether you like it or not and can be played back at any time.

You can hear children scolding each other like parents, for ex ample, 'Don't touch that – mummy says so'. When we feel, think, talk and behave in the way we remember our parents did then we are playing our parent tape. Often it is the parent attitude which shows in later life, rather than the actual words, such as, 'In our line of business the way we do things is...' or 'Leave it up to me...'.

The parent ego is very strongly imprinted on the brain and works automatically, particularly if we are criticized. The critical parent uses words and phrases such as: 'Right and wrong', 'Good and bad', 'What will people say...', 'You must never...', 'Stop that at once...', 'That's the limit!' The helpful or caring parent uses words and phrases such as: 'Oh dear!', 'What a shame...', 'Don't be afraid...', 'Take care...', 'I'll help you...', 'Don't be late', 'It won't take me long to...'. Parents will of course say that they are doing this for our own good.

The child ego

Now while we are soaking up all this parental influence we are in-dulging in being children and a child tape is playing. The child tape has recorded all your emotions, all your early experiences, together with your initial views of yourself and others. The child ego reacts emotionally with the feelings and instincts of childhood.

Child behaviour has two faces. The natural child, who is primi-tive, impulsive, instinctive, undisciplined and demanding and the adapted child, who does as it is told, is polite, sometimes manipula-tive and gives rise to guilt, rebellion, obedience and compromises. Examples of phrases used by the child ego are: 'Let's play', 'I won't', 'It's mine', 'I will in a minute', 'Wow!', 'Let's not be serious, let's party'.

FIGURE 2.1   The ego states

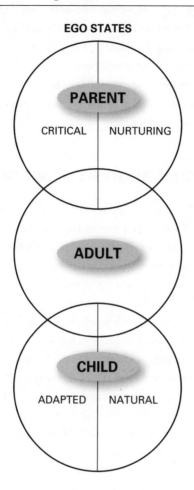

The adult ego

There is a third ego in the Berne theory: the adult.

The adult ego is the mature and deliberating part of your personality. Your actions and words, when this tape is played, are sensible and well-considered, as opposed to the almost automatic reactions of the parent and child egos. The adult ego collects information, evaluates it, works out probabilities, tackles and solves problems, all in an original, calm, collected way. You concentrate on facts, not feelings and prejudices. The adult ego is independent of age. As a rule, the adult ego asks questions and seeks out facts, for example: 'What is that?', 'Let's find out', 'What do you think?', 'Let's experiment', 'Why did that happen?', 'Let's define it', 'What are the choices?', 'How can we handle it best?'

This theory helped me to understand why, after a lifetime's decision not to turn into my mother, I was indeed transmogrified. But why is this theory important to working life?

Transactional analysis at work

At work you will reveal the same behaviour you have experienced and internalized from your parents and also as a child in response to that parental behaviour. If you were told what to do and roundly criticized for doing something rather than being involved in discussion about the pros and cons of actions then you are more likely to be parental at work, telling people what to do, demanding rather than reasoning. In the modern workplace that would be unhelpful. The ultimate end product of such behaviour is being perceived as a bully. So, to reiterate, at work you will behave like your parents unless you make a determined effort to learn new skills.

Alternatively, your adapted child tape may dominate. You immediately go only for politeness and 'niceness' when dealing with a boss or authority figure. As a result, you are perhaps constantly surprised when passed over for promotion. In natural child mode you may decide to take a day off work to enjoy the sunshine and that might be pretty career limiting too.

Being in adult mode at work is the behaviour of choice. Some caring parent and some uninhibited or polite child can be good but not so much that your adult is overwhelmed. So, with limited emotional baggage from the past, you can negotiate calmly, asking questions and responding with equanimity.

Here is some guidance to knowing what behaviour you might be showing.

- Be aware of how your parents behaved towards you.
  Were they critical or nurturing? Which parent do you

take after most? And were you the naughty or polite child
in response?

- Now think about how you deal with authority figures.
  Do you rail against them, capitulate immediately or deal
  with them directly?

- Are you perhaps tough and critical one day, then nice the
  next in compensation? This means you vacillate between
  critical parent and adapted child with no adult in between.

To understand each of the ego states more fully, complete the following quiz.

What tape is playing?

Purpose: To enable you to have a better understanding of which
tapes people are playing so that you can respond accordingly and
thereby achieve smoother communication.

What to do: For each statement below decide whether a parent,
adult or child tape is being played and write P, A or C alongside the
statement to indicate your choice.

---

1 A clerk cannot find an important letter and looks enquiringly
   at a colleague, saying:

   ☐ 'You really ought to be tidier.'

   ☐ 'Ask Mr Anderson, I'm sure he can help you.'

   ☐ 'Don't look at me, I haven't touched it.'

2 There is a rumour during lunch-break that a staff member is being
   moved away from the department. You might say:

   ☐ 'Let's not spread gossip. We haven't heard it officially yet.'

   ☐ 'About time our management saw sense. In my view he should
     have been sacked years ago.'

   ☐ 'That's all we need. They'll fire us tomorrow.'

3 The computer at the check-in counter at the airport isn't working. The operator at the counter might say to the person at the head of the queue:

☐ 'Every time we're busy, it breaks down. If you only knew the problems we have with this thing, every day.'

☐ 'Oh dear, it seems to be temporarily out of action. Never mind, we'll manage some other way.'

☐ 'You wouldn't think it could take the engineer so long to find a simple fault.'

4 A customer has been sitting in a restaurant waiting to be served for some time and points this out to the waiter, who might answer:

☐ 'This is a French restaurant not a fast food cafe. Each dish is specially prepared, you know.'

☐ 'It's not my fault. I keep asking the staff in the kitchen for it.'

☐ 'Thank you for reminding me. I'll see to it straight away.'

Results

Situation one – P A C
Situation two – A P C
Situation three – C A P
Situation four – P C A

How did you do? Look at your answers that diverged from the results and read again the descriptions of parent, adult and child to understand the rationale behind it.

Now you are ready to think about how to react if someone is critically parental towards you. Responding in an equally demanding fashion escalates the interaction into an aggressive encounter. Being polite or trying to make a joke of the authoritarian behaviour may not work either, as 'nice' is ignored, the joke backfires or is seen as inappropriate.

Let me give you an example:

CASE STUDY

A young and very bright advertising agent called Rick gathered a team of young talented staff around him. He was good at choosing the best people in his trade and he was impressive with clients, promising an instant response to their advertising needs. However, back at the office, giving his team these unrealistic timelines, he became demanding and aggressive if they dared to complain. One by one they left. Now he didn't wake up in the morning wondering who he should bully today, but a bully he was. His father was demanding and gave him no praise, as in his father's estimation he never did anything good enough to deserve that praise. His staff became compliant children who were frightened to stand up to him and negotiate better deadlines for projects. Working with him and using the theory of transactional analysis helped him to understand where his autocratic behaviour came from, so when he hired a new team, his communication was much more user-friendly as he calmly asked for their opinion and left his critical parent behind. The company grew exponentially.

I realize that I haven't talked about my father. He died ten years ago. He could certainly, on rare occasions, be the tough parent who produced the rebellious child in me, but more than anything he was the voice of rationality in our small household. He had a light touch with a witty remark and a funny story – sometimes a tad 'Prince Philip' in content but always funny. I remember going to see *Big Fish*, the movie with Ewan McGregor. That film described my father exactly and I cried so much and so long that the cinema staff thought I was staying for the next showing.

So in terms of confidence, the ability I learned from my father was when to choose to be in adult mode, standing back from the situation and asking questions calmly. This has stood me in great stead when there have been crises at work, difficult clients to placate and aggressive staff to motivate. Knowing you can cope calmly with any eventuality is one of the great skills for confidence.

At work there are business plans, marketing plans and IT plans, but when it comes to interacting with those around us, responses are knee-jerk, dependent on upbringing and old learning. Knowing where our behaviour comes from is the first step to changing it and planning what to use when. Some parent behaviour is good when you want to help and support, some child behaviour is fantastic when a celebration is called for, but for confidence in negotiating your ideas and making progress adult mode wins hands down.

Steps to confidence at work

- Think back to how your parents dealt with you and how you responded to them. Are there parallels in your behaviour at work?

- If you are a high critical or nurturing parent at work, cut back on telling and start asking questions. This will immediately put you more in adult mode.

- If you are a high natural or adapted child, reflect on how that may be perceived at work. Fun is wonderful and can be relevant but check whether it is appropriate. Polite or manipulative child behaviour may limit your directness. Practise having open, honest conversations.

- Make a purposeful choice about how to behave. Plan interactions at work in advance and think about when, for example, to be nurturing parent, fun loving or polite child or indeed the calm negotiating adult.

Chapter Three
Albert Bandura's theory of self-efficacy

Although, through a cocktail of nature and nurture, we are like our parents, we can choose to be different. Albert Bandura's theory of self-efficacy is thoroughly optimistic. He says, 'Despite the bad news you hear, the world is full of resilient people who combat drug and alcohol addiction on their own, benefit from hard work and survive traumatic childhoods.' He feels that psychological theory 'grossly over-predicts pathology'.

According to Bandura, if people are given the chance to gain control over their lives, then they can develop the skills to effect changes. They can also learn from looking at how others do things and model this behaviour themselves. It is why we look to people for inspiration, as we want to learn from them how to be successful in whatever we wish to undertake. Self-efficacy, he thinks, is a better term than confidence, which he feels is woolly and nondescript. For our purposes, however, confidence is a more recognized concept.

The inspiration of the red rubber ball

A couple of years ago I met Kevin Carroll, a speaker at a conference I was attending in the United States. He is a wonderful example of Albert Bandura's theory. His father walked out on the family before he was three and his mother took him and his two brothers to stay in a caravan, in a different state hundreds of miles away from his friends and grandparents. After they arrived, his mother told him and his brothers to sit still and behave while she went out to get provisions. The brothers, eight, six and not even four, sat side by side on the bed growing increasingly apprehensive but still not moving. He couldn't remember how long they sat there but it may have been two days. Eventually, driven by hunger, they left the caravan to look for their mother. She never returned.

Holding hands, all three of them made their way to the site office and asked if they could go back home to their grandparents. Luckily, Kevin's grandmother had written her telephone number on his wrist because she knew her daughter's limitations. They were put on a Greyhound bus to take them across three states on condition that their fare would be paid when their grandparents met them at the other end. He remembers them all sitting together in the back seat of the bus, struck dumb by their ordeal.

When they reached their grandparents' house it was a beautiful evening and he asked to play in the park nearby. He found an old burst ball to play with, kicking it from one end of the grass to the other. A gang of local kids arrived with a red rubber ball and he started to play with them. Though small he could run like the wind and they called him 'little fast one'. He played with his new friends most days and as he grew up he became renowned for his speed when playing soccer. This mastery of sport allowed him to join the Air Force to play soccer in Germany but after a damaged knee he became an athletics trainer. Ultimately he was headhunted to be the leader in charge of creativity at Nike.

His passion for sport changed his life. He kept the image of the red rubber ball as his personal symbol of fun and freedom throughout his life. He believes that people should live their dreams and that work can be play if you pursue something you love. What a wonderfully inspirational story and of course not a dry eye in the house.

One of the projects he was involved with at Nike was the placement of a huge red rubber ball the size of a small office block at various strategic points in Portland Oregon. He showed us footage of a film they made of the inhabitants' responses. Children loved the huge red ball poking and prodding it, bouncing off it, scrambling up the sides of it. They interacted with the ball. Adults, on the other hand, would walk past and apart from glancing sideways briefly with a swivel of the eyes, studiously ignored its presence. Were they used to oversized red rubber balls taking over their city? You would have thought so. The film was revelatory about how, when we reach so-called maturity, we lose the marvellous childlike qualities of open wonderment and fun. In transactional analysis terms, a bit of natural child is essential to maintain an enquiring mind and a sense of enjoyment.

Afterwards I waited in a queue for him to sign his book. It was a long queue but he was just as interested in the people at the back of that queue as he had been with those at the front. He asked questions, made suggestions and personalized everything he wrote. In him I saw energy, optimism and a love of humanity. On my book he wrote that I had to continue to 'dream big' and with the launch of my coaching school I have indeed taken his advice on board. So dreaming big works!

Getting control of your life

I was never a confident child – despite my loving upbringing, partly because being an only child I lacked the rough and tumble of a large family, and partly because of being over-analytical in solitude. If I lacked confidence as a child, this was nothing to the angst I felt as a teenager. Spots, specs and being a singer never seemed cool enough at school, but at university, psychology and contact lenses worked wonders for my self-esteem.

My professor of psychology was a strange little fellow who looked like a thinner version of Einstein, with the jerky movements of a puppet. I was never sure if he cultivated the nutty professor look on purpose or arrived at it by default. He was, though, inspirational about the true purpose of psychologists as observers and experimenters, as people watchers and inter-actors. As a shy first-year student, I would take my book with me to the canteen and read as I ate so that no one would notice me. This changed radically after being adjured by the Prof to be people watchers and observers of human behaviour. I learned to sit with my back to the wall so that I could view the room and look at everyone who walked past or sat at adjacent tables. The study of body language was not as prevalent then as it is now, with 'experts' on reality television, so this study was very new to us. The interesting part of it was that by not focusing on me, my beating heart and blushing face, I became other-focused with a different purpose. From that day in the university canteen, I grew in confidence.

This concept of being 'other' focused is a powerful one for confidence. As you forget about yourself and concentrate on those around you, anxiety lessens and confidence increases. When I was working on one of the first reality television series, *Confidence Lab*, there were twelve participants lacking in confidence who had to be turned around in seven days.

The overriding impression I gained as the week progressed was of wildly self-oriented people obsessed with their own internal torments, caring not a fig for anyone else. Getting them to think about relationships in that group so that they could help each other and create action plans to gain control over their lives, took the focus off themselves and immediately increased their confidence.

After my first degree I had a brief sojourn as a social worker in Greenock. This really did not suit me. I liked my clients but I railed against how taxpayers' money was spent. There seemed to me little rationale for setting up projects with no evaluation of success or failure. Greenock had huge areas of poverty, so clearly help was necessary, but was there any piloting of different options for consideration? None that I could see. Psychology had taught me too well. I hadn't realized that I wanted to be part of a caring profession that was totally grounded in good theory and practice. In fact it surprised me that evidence-based delivery was important to me at all. I pursued an offer to become a clinical psychologist and my life changed.

Choosing a career is often a matter of trial and error. Only by jumping in can you determine what works for you. However, jumping out when you realize your mistake is equally important. So many people get stuck in the wrong jobs for their skills and personalities and continue to have unfulfilled lives. This erodes confidence and limits success. Don't let that happen to you.

Steps to confidence at work

- Realize that despite your background or upbringing you can change to be who you want to be.
- Dream big.
- Become 'other' focused. It removes the spotlight from you and increases confidence.
- Jump in to try out jobs but be prepared to jump out if they are unsuitable or unfulfilling for you.

Chapter Four
Martin Seligman's learned optimism

My next epiphany was during a British Psychological Society conference in Edinburgh. Martin Seligman was talking about positive thinking. I knew it was important therapeutically but had not made any personal connections. And remember, I was dealing with very dysfunctional patients, helping them to leave the house or hold down a job after years of unemployment as a result of depression. How was this applicable to me?

Seligman supplied evidence of a longitudinal study he had undertaken in which he benchmarked a large group of people as optimists or pessimists based on the language they used during telephone calls, in letters and memos and in their coffee room chat, and then followed them up over 20 years. The results were compelling. There were more positive thinkers alive at the end of the project than pessimists. Optimists were also more likely to be successful in all that they undertook, were less likely to have nasty life events and were less likely to become depressed. That was it for me. Optimism was not for 'other people', this was what I needed. I required the evidence that it worked. You get so used to the thinking style you employ because it is inside your head with no external repudiation. I was definitely a half empty person who used little phrases like 'With my luck I will fail' when sitting exams or 'With my luck I will forget my words' when I was singing. I saw myself as accident prone rather than someone who coped whatever the adversity.

Humour

My sense of humour was also embedded in messing up. It was about me as silly; a 'screwer- up' who could recount numerous examples of saying the wrong thing or falling over at important moments.

These humorous self put-downs followed me into work when recounting stories as I delivered leadership courses. I found myself choosing examples that revealed me as a failure, not as masterful. When relinquishing negativity this was one of the most difficult parts to change but I realized that I had to be a role model for others and lead the way for participants' success. Falling about was not inspirational. New stories were found.

When coaching clients I am aware of the same tendency in others for personal put-downs and, while it might be endearing in a social context, it reveals a singular lack of confidence at work. If you use humour in that way then do change. It often reveals itself at the beginning of presentations with comments like 'Sorry I didn't have time to prepare...', 'Try following that' after the performance by another good speaker, or even 'Bear with me as I really hate speaking in public'.

The Seligman quote below gives us the expectation of change.

Habits of thinking need not be forever. One of the most significant findings in psychology in the last twenty years is that individuals can choose the way they think.

Martin Seligman from *Learned Optimism*

The questionnaire below will help you discover your thinking style. We can talk about the results afterwards. Just tick either A or B in each case. This is an adaptation of a much longer Seligman questionnaire.

Origins of Optimism Questionnaire

1 You forgot a friend's birthday
  A I'm not good at remembering birthdays
  B I was preoccupied with other things

2 You run for a community post and get it
  A I devote a lot of time and energy to campaigning
  B I work hard at everything I do

3 You get lost driving to a friend's house
  A I missed a turn
  B My friend gave me bad directions

4 You are frequently asked to dance at a party
  A I am outgoing at parties
  B I was in perfect form that night

5 You miss an important engagement
  A Sometimes my memory fails me
  B I sometimes forget to check my diary

6 The project you are in charge of is a great success
  A I kept a close watch over everyone's work
  B Everyone devoted a lot of time and energy to it

7 You gain weight over the holidays and you can't lose it
  A Diets don't work in the long run
  B The diet I tried didn't work

8 A friend thanks you for getting him through a bad time
  A I enjoy helping him through tough times
  B I care about people

9 You buy your partner a present and they don't like it
  A I don't put enough thought into things like that
  B They have very picky tastes

10 You are asked to head up an important project
  A I have just successfully completed another similar project
  B I am a good supervisor

11 You lose at a sporting event for which you have been training for a long time
  A I'm not very athletic
  B I'm not good at that sport

12 You tell a joke and everyone laughs
  A My timing was perfect
  B The joke was funny

FIGURE 4.1 Origins of optimism questionnaire scoring

Optimism type	Optimist choice	Your choice
1 sometimes thinking for bad events	B	
2 everywhere thinking for good events	B	
3 not me thinking for bad events	B	
4 always thinking for good events	A	
5 specific thinking for bad events	B	
6 me thinking for good events	A	
7 sometimes thinking for bad events	B	
8 everywhere thinking for good events	B	
9 not me thinking for bad events	B	
10 always thinking for good events	B	
11 specific thinking for bad events	B	
12 me thinking for good events	A	
Total matches		

Transfer your As and Bs from the 12 questions into the blank right hand spaces of Figure 4.1.

Learned optimism

Seligman's theory of learned optimism revolves around three thinking styles: persistence, pervasiveness and personalization, or as I call it, always, everywhere and me thinking. When good things happen to optimists they think that they are on a roll and this will not be confined to one area of their lives. It will generalize to everything they do and it is very much due to them.

Pessimists experience the complete opposite. They think that only sometimes, in very specific circumstances, will they succeed and it is usually down to other people's involvement. Any success is attributed to a fluke and may never happen again.

Looking back at the 12 questions, you can see how optimists and pessimists have opposite interpretations of bad events. Pessimists think that when bad things happen they are on the slippery slope to disaster with every aspect of their life affected and it is entirely their fault. Contrarily, optimists think that a bad event is but 'a mere glitch and they will be fine in a moment...and anyway loads of people were involved in that screw-up not just me.'

Review your score. Well done for the areas in which you are optimistic and take note of those you need to work on. Check out the nature of the statement. Were your negative scores around always, everywhere, or me concepts? People are often surprised by this questionnaire as they may have viewed themselves as positive thinkers but achieve a low score here. The major area is the 'me' section. You may be optimistic about events but shy away from patting yourself on the back for successes or beat yourself up with blame when things go wrong.

Participants on my Leadership Programme often complain that it would be arrogant to say that you have played a major part in successes. Surely it is about celebrating a team effort, all for one and one for all. Of course it would be good leadership to reward the team, but you can still tell yourself that you were the main coordinator/contributor. In the still of the night you can smile and feel good.

Having discovered that I was optimistic about my patients but not about myself, my life or my work, I realized I had much to change. First to go was what I said to myself all the time, my inner dialogue. Out went 'with my luck I will mess up..', in came a little phrase that worked for me, 'I'm OK' not 'I'm fabulous' or 'I'm the best', but 'I'm OK'. Anything more seemed overinflated to my Scottish psyche.

Every morning I would sit at the end of my bed visualizing the day ahead. For example, it is 10 am and my first meeting is finished and has gone well; it is now midday and my presentation to the board of the bank has been successful and they want additional coaching for 20 staff; lunch with the partners and they are discussing the successful allocation of the project to my company... and so on. As a result of this hard work, sitting on the edge of the bed every morning for three weeks, I now rarely imagine anything going wrong in my life or work. And if it does, I know I will cope.

Three thinking styles

- Always
- Everywhere
- Me

Thinking for good events

- Pessimists think that sometimes, in specific circumstances, they might succeed and 'it's probably a fluke'.
- Optimists think that always, in every part of their life, they will succeed and 'it's all due to me'.

Thinking for bad events

- Pessimists think that always, in every part of their life, they will fail in some way and 'it's all my fault'.
- Optimists think that sometimes, in some circumstances, they might fare less well and 'it may be nothing to do with me'.

Steps to confidence at work

- Be aware of 'always', 'everywhere' and 'me' thinking.
- When things go well there is no reason why they should not continue to go well.
- You are part of the success around you.
- Tell yourself that you are OK.
- Visualize success every day.

Chapter Five
HJ Eysenck's theory of extraversion–introversion

It might seem obvious to those who know me that I am extraverted; I love people, love parties, in fact I love anything to do with gregariousness. However, I despised what I saw as the shallowness of extraversion and wanted nothing more than to be a contemplative introvert. HJ Eysenck, the celebrated psychologist, saved me from myself, declaring the extraversion–introversion dimension of personality as genetic. So since there was nothing to be done about it I could simply concentrate on being a happy extravert.

Extraversion does have an impact on jobs pursued and life partners chosen. I completed some research on Borstal boys for my postgraduate degree in clinical psychology, using Eysenck's personality measure. Eighty-nine per cent of my research group were extraverted and I came to understand the absurdity of locking up in solitary cells extraverted young men who needed the constant presence and stimulation of others. Of course this desire for stimulation may have led to their thieving and lawless behaviour in the first place. Putting them to good use, providing them with the distractions of education or skills training, is not just for their rehabilitation to an outside world but for their compliance to the inside one of prison.

I discovered that I needed like-minded people to work with and that the relatively solitary pursuits of laboratory research and experimentation were not for me. I needed people and people to help. This was my *raison d'être*.

Discover for yourself whether you are extraverted or introverted by completing the following short questionnaire. Mark whether you agree or disagree with the statements listed; add up your points at the end.

FIGURE 5.1   Extraversion–introversion questionnaire

	Agree	Disagree
I am the life and soul of the party.		
I enjoy being the centre of attention.		
I am skilled in handling social situations.		
I like to be where the action is.		
I make new friends easily.		
I am quiet around strangers.		
I don't like to draw attention to myself.		
I don't like to party at weekends.		
I like to work independently.		
I often enjoy spending time by myself.		
Score		

Results

For the first five questions agreement indicates a tendency towards extraversion, while for the last five, agreement indicates introversion.

Extraversion

Extraversion is 'the act, state, or habit of being predominantly concerned with and obtaining gratification from what is outside the self'. Extraverts tend to enjoy human interactions, tending to be enthusiastic, talkative, assertive and gregarious. They take pleasure in activities that involve large social gatherings, such as parties, community activities, public demonstrations and business or political groups. Politics, teaching, sales, managing, brokering and acting are fields that favour extraversion.

Extraverted people are likely to enjoy time spent with others and find less reward in time spent alone. They tend to be energized when around others and they are more prone to boredom when they are by themselves. They speak spontaneously and often.

Introversion

Introversion is 'the state of or tendency towards being wholly or predominantly concerned with and interested in one's own mental life'. Introverts tend to be more reserved and less outspoken in large groups. They often take pleasure in solitary activities such as reading, writing, drawing and using computers. The archetypal artist, writer, sculptor, engineer, composer and inventor are all highly introverted. Introverts are likely to enjoy time spent alone and find less reward in time spent with large groups of people, though they tend to enjoy interactions with close friends. They prefer to concentrate on a single activity at a time and like to observe situations before they participate. Introverts are easily overwhelmed by too much stimulation from social gatherings. They are more analytical before speaking.

Introversion is not the same as shyness. Introverts choose solitary over social activities from preference, whereas shy people avoid social encounters out of fear.

The world needs both introverts and extraverts. The extravert getting a meeting going with everyone contributing, the introvert summarizing quietly and moving the discussion forward in ways not envisaged. So many of my clients who are quieter and more studious want to be extraverted and ask to be coached to become more outgoing. I always refuse. They can become bolder in their opinions, sharper in their presentation skills or more interested in the well-being of their staff, but they must celebrate being an introvert and what that means for their contribution at work. This of course is the nature of confidence.

Why is it that the extravert seems more valued at work than the introvert in our society? A little more quiet reflection at the top of some of our institutions would have limited our exposure on the money markets. Listening to all around you, not just those who speak most or are in agreement, is a forgotten leadership skill. Business leaders often want compliance rather than challenge and that limits company growth and the confidence of employees to find their voice.

Steps to confidence at work

- Determine whether you are an extravert or an introvert.
- Does the work you have chosen suit this personality trait? If not, plan for change.
- Be happy with who you are.
- Respect differences in others.
- Learn to speak up about your ideas, regardless of personality type.

Chapter Six
Friedman and Rosenman's theory of Type A and Type B behaviours

A nother lifesaver of a theory is Type A and Type B behaviours instituted by Friedman and Rosenman. They were cardiologists who noticed that the front of their waiting room chairs needed reupholstering but not the back. A quick appraisal of a full surgery revealed a lot of anxious people literally on the edges of their seats. They then researched the nature of anxiety and hard driving behaviour and the relationship of these to coronary heart disease. They called this Type A behaviour. More relaxed and sociable behaviour was Type B. Now this initial research has been challenged as it did not take into account genetic differences as a variable and other researchers only found anger and hostility as measures correlating with heart disease. I have no doubt, though, that driving for results at the expense of all else, feeling under constant pressure and regularly working long hours, not only make for dull boys and girls but will also give rise to increased anger and hostility.

Anger

As part of a BBC television programme, *All the Rage*, I was asked, as is the way with these things, to change an angry man in a day.

Let's call him Richard. He was perfectly pleasant with me but told me details of his 'short fuses' at home that had me wondering how his relationships survived at all. His father had never been happy with his accomplishments and he was constantly trying to prove himself. When I travelled as a passenger in his car to get to one of the filming locations, I was amazed at the imprecations showered upon unsuspecting pedestrians and drivers. He was angry with anyone daring to be in front of him on the road. His aim apparently was to be king of a completely clear road. Not an achievable goal in London at any time, really.

I started by challenging his thinking and asking first what might be behind his disgust with pedestrians. He felt they were wilfully walking in front of his car. I suggested he envisage what kind of day they might be having and asked him for alternative explanations for their behaviour on the road. He grudgingly admitted that they might be worried about work or a loved one and didn't notice his approach. We then proceeded through cars and white vans, the latter producing the most invective. He eventually admitted that they might not be concentrating for a variety of reasons and that probably he could 'cut them some slack' and think differently about those around him on the road.

Next we focused on relaxation and breathing more slowly so that his anxiety threshold was raised and therefore his anger triggered less often. We talked about how he could practise this relaxation at home so that when his partner spoke he listened rather than jumping to conclusions with an angry retort.

For me, the major thing in all of this is that our own anger damages us more than it damages anyone else and it is of little consequence whether we are right or wrong – it still wreaks havoc with our nervous systems. When someone becomes angry very quickly the physical reactions can cause the blood to clot speedily and this can travel to the heart and lungs. Pretty serious when combined with a drop in blood oxygen levels. In addition, as if this weren't enough, anger creates stomach acids that can cause irritable bowel disease, diarrhoea and stomach ulcers. For people like Richard, constantly angry most days, there is a risk of long-term high blood pressure, which could cause angina.

A rating scale for anger

I suggested that Richard rate the causes of his anger on a scale of 1 to 10 and if only a 1, he should relax and let things go. If a 10 (perhaps a man in a balaclava with sawn-off shotgun threatening him) then he could allow himself to be angry. Anger is such a powerful emotion that it should be used sparingly and only when we are in really life-threatening situations. A rating scale helps by distancing you from the emotion. I suggest to my clients that they should not be angry more than twice a year. They often ask if they can save up for a really big blowout if not using their yearly quota. The answer is no.

I had forgotten when *All the Rage* was going to be scheduled, so one night after returning home late I was flicking channels and heard a voice I recognized saying that he was more confident that he could handle his anger better and how that had changed his relationships.

So I include Type A and Type B behaviours in my shopping basket of self-revelatory theories as it helped me discover that you can have control over your emotions and therefore your behaviour. As soon as I heard about the physiological effects of anger and hostility I stopped being an angry person. Why should someone else's stupidity shorten your life by hours, minutes or even seconds? Now the only people to get a 5 on my rating scale are security officers at airports, who have been given a tiny piece of authority and, boy, are they going to use it. Deep breaths work for me when standing in line and a deep thankfulness that they are keeping us safe from harm.

Steps to confidence at work

- If you are a hard-driving person at work find time at weekends to relax.

- In fact, relax at work.

- Rate your anger on a scale of 1 to 10; under 5 let it go; above 5 talk about how you feel to whoever generated the anger.

- Limit any angry outbursts to two a year.

Chapter Seven
Life's rich tapestry

Of course many experiences have increased my confidence. University helped, as I came to understand that I wasn't as stupid as I thought I might be. And discovering psychology as a profession has certainly provided me with a lifetime's motivation and stimulation.

Barlinnie Prison

I remember having to complete a forensic psychology placement at Barlinnie Prison in Glasgow. They were piloting a Special Unit there that had five murderers in it. The purpose of this unit was to see if the worst offenders could be rehabilitated by means of individual and group counselling as well as by art therapies and further education. The most notorious alumnus of the Special Unit was Jimmy Boyle, an infamous murderer from the Gorbals, an equally infamous part of Glasgow, now completely remodelled.

Having access to talk to these feared men was, and here I am searching for the right adjective, humbling. Nothing of course excuses their behaviour, but being given the opportunity to listen and to understand why it might have happened was beyond compare. Jimmy's life, in the violent Gorbals, was kill or be killed, and since he was cleverer than most, he dominated the local crime scene. He was caught and sent to prison at Peterhead; he talked to me about life in solitary confinement. At Christmas, he and the other prisoners would steal spoons from dinner and start to dig their way out. Of course none of them got further than damaging a little grouting round some bricks, but for them it was trying to do something to gain control.

He wrote his much-acclaimed book *A Sense of Freedom*, and on being freed never returned to prison, which flew in the face of much public opinion. His time in the Special Unit had changed him irrevocably. My abiding memory was teaching him to bake a chocolate cake to my mother's recipe in the prison kitchen. Jimmy Boyle in an apron was an unusual sight indeed.

There are some other events and encounters that have been seminal in building my confidence.

Entrepreneurship

Starting my own company was a thrill as well as a risk. Having only yourself and your skills to rely on is scary, but looking back, it does build confidence. For all you budding entrepreneurs out there, I didn't leave the NHS day job immediately. I had the idea of setting up a private practice working evenings and weekends and then built it up for a couple of years before leaving my day job. Even then, I worked part-time on a nightly television news programme before I took the leap. So it was a gradual process for me that beat jumping off the cliff without a parachute.

An option for you might be to start your own company. If you have an idea for a business, do some research and see if, like me, you can start gradually working from home. Then, if it looks like a winner, you can perhaps work at it part-time till you generate enough income to run your business full time.

I certainly found it helped with confidence-building as I found myself speaking at conferences and even delivering after dinner speeches as a result of setting up in business.

Finding your voice

Writing books was also something I never thought I would achieve. Finding your voice and having a view of the world, or your bit of it, is another stage of building confidence. When I was a child of four I was interviewed by the headmaster to be admitted to Jordanhill College School in Glasgow. My mother was keen for me to get in as it was close to home. She sat behind me, willing me to say the right thing. I had other ideas. So when I was asked if I wanted to attend this school, I said, without hesitation, 'Oh no, I am going to the same school as the girl across the road, thank you very much.' Unfazed, he commented that I certainly knew my own mind and offered me a place, much to my mother's relief.

So it is worth thinking back to when you found your voice, spoke up to defend your position or pursued an idea. It was a question I asked my 20 participants and received various replies. Andi Keeling found her voice at age 3, others such as Rosalyn Rahme also gave her opinion when young but mentioned that speaking up while understanding another's position is a more sophisticated way of vocalizing our thoughts. That came at a later age for her. I think she mentioned age 40.

During my teenage years I lost my directness and became compliant in my desire to fit in, only emerging with a semblance of confidence in my late twenties. I then went through that phase where I told it how it was, the unembellished truth as I saw it, sparing no blushes with a glorious righteous indignation. Looking back, how insufferable I must have been. Some people get stuck at this stage of communication, mistaking outspoken arrogance for confidence. This 'child' behaviour is, however, very different from the 'adult' version of standing up for yourself or a principle in a way that does not alienate those around you but leads to a compromise win–win agreement. That is a set of much higher order skills, very much what Rosalyn Rahme was talking about. We will discuss this more in Part 3 about influencing and networking.

My confidence role models

We all have our role models who have influenced us. My list, though not complete, follows.

> Aaron Beck, the father of cognitive psychology, I admired for his overwhelming interest in people and his warm and rewarding nature. He must have been in his late seventies when I met him but still as sharp as a tack.
>
> Tom Peters for his chutzpah on winning Speaker of the Year from the Speakers Club of America, I think it was. He went through their manifesto point by point and claimed to do nothing of what they suggested. He said that he just told stories about people and organizations.
>
> Tony Buzan for bringing us Mind Mapping™. How anyone can work without using Mind Maps is beyond me and the utility of this technique will be discussed later in the book. To be able to plan your discourse or the input to a meeting quickly and effectively is a major skill for confidence.
>
> Bill Clinton for his relaxation and charisma. Seeing him speak in the Albert Hall a few years ago was mesmerizing. Regardless of his personal life, there stood a man in front of that huge auditorium who was secure in the knowledge of what he had brought and was bringing to the world. He was utterly confident.

Your confidence role models

It is worth noting your favourites and, of more importance, what you are going to do to replicate the bits of them you admire. Make a list, ascribing the attributes you applaud or envy and add some actions about how you could change to become more confident like them.

You don't have to like everything about them. Choose the bits that are relevant to your confidence.

Steps to confidence at work

- Think back over all your life experiences and pinpoint the ones which increased your confidence. Do more of these.

- Reflect on when you found your voice. Speaking up about beliefs is a major skill for confidence. When you are heard, it encourages you to speak up more.

- Replicate the confident behaviour of your role models.

Part Two
Branding for confidence

Chapter Eight
Bird's eye view
of branding

Confidence is like the two-headed Janus: one part internal, one part external. Much of confidence is inside your head, knowing who you are, understanding your strengths, thinking positively about what you do and the situation you are in. It is also about selling yourself externally and having the language to do that elegantly. So Part 2 is about the contemplation of your public persona and what that might look like, understanding the impact you make on first meeting, finding words to describe your skills and absolutely knowing what kind of work would suit you as a person. In other words, just like a product, you need a brand.

Brand has so many meanings and connotations; to burn with an iron to indicate ownership, to stigmatize, to accuse or condemn, to mark with a trademark. What we are talking about here is something more akin to trademarking.

'Branding you' means finding a unique combination of words employed in creating an image that identifies you and differentiates you from your competitors. Over time, this image becomes associated with a level of credibility in other people's minds. You will want to be known as standing for certain benefits and values and therefore be desirable as a colleague and partner.

So Part 2 will deliver the following:

- What your potential customers might want – what CEOs and recruiters are looking for in an employee.

- An exploration of what would provide you with career satisfaction: skills, passions, values, lifestyle and environment. All leading to a more confident you.

- Your leadership style and what your natural contribution to work will be. This helps with a vocabulary you can use to describe what you do best.

- Stories – what are the stories you tell about what you do?

- Benefits: how exciting might you be to work with, how user friendly to your team, colleagues and boss and the hard benefits – what profit or return for their money are they getting from working with you?

- You as a product – what would you be like if you were a car or a colour?

- Your brand slogan – defining it for use with customers, clients and contacts in one sentence.

Business branding

Knowing what you are good at, what you are truly passionate about and therefore what you represent as a brand makes the difference between success and failure in today's market. Let's look at branding in business first, as we are more familiar with that concept.

CASE STUDY

I recently met a young entrepreneur, Fraser Doherty, who started his own jam company when he was 15. Jam is seen nowadays as an unhealthy product with too many calories, so he developed a formula for organic jams with fruit, fruit juice and no sugar. He called this product SuperJam. He is now 21, has numerous awards for his entrepreneurship and has featured in *Forbes* magazine. He and his small team went round supermarkets to get customers to taste his product and received feedback as to what they wanted. In terms of values, passion and lifestyle, Fraser loves his work and, alongside his business, runs a charity providing afternoon tea parties for the isolated elderly. Everyone in SuperJam is involved in the charity. His story is learning jam-making from his grandmother and selling his products to neighbours until he found a supermarket that encouraged him to return when he could manufacture in bulk. He did return and the rest is history.

So the SuperJam brand is natural, rejuvenated and giving.

With someone like Fraser Doherty, he is so associated with his company that the SuperJam Brand is him and he is SuperJam. He is natural, young and caring just like his product. So your brand will be associated with your work especially if, like Fraser, you love what you do. Despite his youth, he is supremely confident and robustly positive as he says 'I know I am doing the right thing for me'.

CASE STUDY

There was a Scottish fashion retailer who was very successful at selling inexpensive clothing. Often she would have expensive designers' labels that were perhaps end of season or had the tiniest of flaws invisible to the naked eye, at a fraction of the cost. So, as you could imagine, there were queues of women clamouring for her bargains and she must have made a fortune. She had a great brand. She really wanted to be upmarket though and sank her cash into a very expensive shop selling diamante evening gowns in the best street in town.... and went bust in a year. Her passion and expertise was 'value for money', not 'top end'. She mixed brands and failed.

We love brands like Coke, Heinz, Virgin, Starbucks, Armani, M&S, Topshop, iPhone, to name a few. These brands enable marketing and the sale of large amounts of product. We know what they stand for. Owners and shareholders are very protective of their brand because if it is sullied then sales are affected and business may cease – the best example is Gerald Ratner who destroyed his jewellery brand over dinner when he called it the equivalent of cheap and cheerful. Those who bought their wedding rings there did not want their very personal shopping experience and, by implication, their relationship so described.

Despite my early desire to be an academic, what I now realize I do best is to translate psychological theory into easy concepts to help others transform themselves. I am definitely at the populist end of the literary spectrum but with a good bit of intellectual credibility because of my background as a psychologist. So that self-examination about what and how I like to write fuels the branding of me and my work.

For my book *Fast Track to the Top*, I interviewed 80 CEOs and what had a major impact on me was how they knew their strengths and leveraged them to great effect. They were not all things to all people. They knew how to sell their positives and what they could deliver in the workplace and had assimilated all of that into a confident personal brand.

First impressions

So let's start to brand you with confidence.

When you are meeting people for the first time at work, when you are networking with people outside your organization or being interviewed for a post that means promotion, the most important part of confident communication is to have an impact on those you want to impress and a vocabulary to describe who you are and what you do.

This chapter provides you with feedback about what recruiters and CEOs are looking for in a successful candidate. There will be challenging questions to help you discover what you truly want from a career. In addition, I will look at how you can market your skills to the people and organizations you would like to target. All of these actions increase your confidence at work and help you to build a successful career.

The results of my random interviews with those who might want to hire you were interesting as to what they are looking for in a candidate for promotion.

Rosalyn Rahme of Goldjobs, an Executive Search Company

She wants candidates who have nothing to prove, who are relaxed enough to allow those around them to be successful. People who are prickly or prudish are a 'no go' in her estimation. She had many comments to make about Generation Y. She felt that people under 30 need to cope with critical feedback at work and not just walk away when the going gets tough. Nowadays, alternative jobs are not thick on the ground.

Angela Middleton, top recruiter with Middleton Murray

She looks for signs of a good work ethic with determination to get the job done and flexibility to be open to change. She disagreed with Rosalyn Rahme and said that young people were worried about the job situation and wanted nothing more than to stay in a job. Angela mentioned appearance as a major determining factor. She looked for a clean, fresh, workmanlike image with good eye contact, a smiling demeanour and a firm handshake. She would also like candidates to ask questions, show interest in the organization and have done some background research – taking control rather than appearing like a victim.

Andi Keeling, Head of Learning at the Royal Bank of Scotland

She told me that on first meeting someone, especially a new recruit, she would look for poised body language, a calm, friendly and positive approach, assertion without aggression. She wants to see evidence of well-structured and influential communication, and for her the true sign of confidence – being unafraid of silence.

She says, 'When recruiting staff, what I look for in addition to specific expertise is a positive attitude every time! A drive and desire to do a great job together with a keen and genuine interest in what is required. I can always teach someone what to do and how to do it, but I can't give them a great attitude or drive and personal commitment'.

Brian Lang, former CEO and University Vice Chancellor

He says that at a first meeting he values an ability to get straight to the point with a 'lack of flannel'. When conversing, he is also looking for signs of emotional intelligence. At work he is concerned to see a willingness to embrace and contribute to the team. He has made mistakes when recruiting in the past and believes a wrong hire at senior levels can be thoroughly destructive to a top team, taking huge amounts of time and energy to correct.

Tari Lang, CEO of a Branding Organization in Dubai and executive coach

She notices eye contact and handshake first when meeting someone but is also looking for contribution early on in conversation. People have got to be interested and interesting she says and that should happen from the get go. That interest should reveal itself in body language; sitting or standing forward not shifting around or backing off.

*

I also spoke to two young entrepreneurs, Fraser Doherty, the young founder of SuperJam, and Oli Norman of DADA PR about what would impress them on first meeting someone and what they would want in a new hire.

Fraser Doherty, Founder and MD of SuperJam

He started making jam with his grandmother's recipe and by age 16 started producing sufficient quantities for Waitrose to stock it. Side by side with his company, he has a charity that serves after-noon teas (with his jam of course) in community centres for the elderly living on their own. These afternoon teas are now happening throughout the UK.

He notices when someone is friendly, open and funny with good conversation. He is also impressed by a willingness to challenge the status quo. When recruiting staff he is keen to see a sense of fun and caring, with a candidate asking lots of relevant questions. All at SuperJam must work with the afternoon teas so they must love the concept and just love what they do.

Oli Norman of DADA, a PR company

He has an interesting take on events and publicity. He took a double-decker bus to Paris and parked it illegally under the Eiffel Tower, and then used Facebook to get Scottish football supporters to gather round the bus. 20,000 turned up. On another occasion he persuaded the imbibers at the opening of a new bar in Glasgow to take off their clothes for a publicity photograph. The photograph was a great success on the internet as you can imagine.

Oli is in his twenties. At first meeting he looks for a positive energy, absolutely no 'mood hoovers', as he calls negative, under-mining people. 'You can tell in the first minute, then it's down to experience and credibility,' he says. What you are looking for in an employee is 'someone with whom you can have an open conversation. It's difficult to get a job in my company and it's difficult to keep it'.

He was always confident himself, so he looks for that in others. He claims he was always a 'wee shit' with an ability to push himself. He believes that you need to seek out opportunities to become confident. He went to the West coast of America by himself to work when he was 15 and expects others who want to work with him to have taken similar risks in their background.

Tom DiPuma, a renowned US salesman of global standing

He gave me the following response about meeting people who might become colleagues for the first time.

> When I first meet someone I look for them to ask clarifying questions on points that are complex or require supporting information as

that demonstrates engagement and interest. Soliciting alternative theories or explanations shows openness to constructive criticism and willingness to risk defending a point of view.

In someone's thinking belief is one thing. Being willing to challenge underlying assumptions and/or the logic of a recommendation, belief or position shows confidence – not just in the belief, but in the integrity of the process someone went through to arrive at their conclusions.

In terms of emotions, anger, fear, elation – all create energy. Positive emotion and enthusiasm in common goals creates focus and helps a vision of success. Negative emotions can halt rational discourse.

I look to see evidence of respect for the points of view of others and the willingness to explain beliefs and adjust them for new facts or ideas, that they will change their view or position if justified.

I also want to see evidence that 'you are in the business'. This is revealed by the work or project that brought the most satisfaction. What was it about that event that was special? Can you tell a simple, yet compelling story about an accomplishment in your business? Do your eyes light up?

Tony Buzan, the creator of Mind Mapping™

I met Tony recently at a conference where we were both speaking. He spared me some time to talk about what would make a good first impression on him.

At first meeting I notice whether there is openness in mind and body, a willingness to make contact and a joy in taking risks. In someone's thinking I am looking for originality, a fast learner who delights in the unknown. And emotionally I want someone who is excited and exciting but calm if that is not too dichotomous. As for their behaviour, the enthusiastically social, the witty and those who laugh more than average will make an impact on me. And at interview I am looking for a love of the task, energy, stamina, with supporting stories evidencing all of that and a light in the eye.

So the eyes have it! And what they are describing in summary is confidence.

This is important feedback for you from these successful people about what gets their attention. So do take it seriously. The distillation for me is around energy, 'a light in the eye' and an inquisitiveness about life and business.

Steps to confidence at work

- Being aware of how you look, what you wear and the poise of your body language.

- Showing a positive attitude by asking questions, being interested and having interesting things to say.

- Having great interpersonal skills, being friendly, open and funny.

- Being energetic, excited by work and revealing that with bright eyes and a ready smile.

Steps to confidence at work

Chapter Nine
Great expectations

Let me nail my colours to the mast. I don't think you can be confident at work if you are in a job that does not suit your talents, one you find boring or turns you into a silent, compliant slave.

We all expect something from our jobs. For some it might be money, for others a chance to fulfil potential. It is important to define what it is you want from your work, your colleagues, management and, most importantly, from yourself. A big mistake is to think that a job is only about a pay packet, important though that may be. If you just go for the money, then you may hop from job to similar job in the pursuit of a slightly better pay offer without realizing that there are other ingredients that would inspire and stimulate you.

George was a bright young man whose parents divorced when he was a teenager. Filled with angst and anger he escaped the clutches of the education system and left, with few qualifications. He worked out that he would earn most by joining a call centre. Initially he was challenged by the job but after six months he was bored because he was actually a fast learner. Rather than staying to pursue a promotion, he left and joined another call centre for slightly more money. Of course, after six months he got bored again. He went through this pattern four times without realizing he needed a career plan that was not just dependent on small monetary increments. Eventually he went back to college and completed a marketing diploma. When I met him a few months ago the difference in his demeanour was tangible. He looked me in the eye instead of a sideways glance, his posture was erect and he smiled. He looked confident.

What are you looking for?

So what are you looking for from work? The results from an IPSO-Reid Globe and Mail survey show the following:

- Work–life balance – 41 per cent.
- Level of responsibility of work – 27 per cent.
- Challenge of job – 27 per cent.
- Salary level – 25 per cent.
- Loyalty from your team or those who report to you – 25 per cent.
- Amount of vacation time – 4 per cent.
- Title of role – 4 per cent.

So the question for you is: are you getting what you want from work? If not, why not? It is a key question to ask yourself and a tougher one to answer honestly. Sometimes it can be challenging to understand the complexity of what is happening in your situation. The next section helps you to explore your options.

So answer the following questions:

1 What is it that you want from work? Rank your list in order, starting with what you want the most.

2 What is it you don't want from work?

3 What is your definition of 'career success'?

4 What is your ideal job?

It is important to consider your career from all aspects of your life. Several studies have shown that fewer than 2 in 10 people use a decision-making strategy that addresses how their decisions fit into all phases of their life, including those that appear unrelated. Those who sacrifice their individual beliefs and backgrounds ultimately express one-third less satisfaction with their jobs and almost two-thirds less satisfaction with their lives. Low job and life satisfaction correlate highly with low confidence.

The career confidence formula

So a formula for a confident working life is below. Answer the questions attached to each part of the equation and you will realize that work is a complex meshing of these components.

$$Skills + Passions + Values + Lifestyle + Environment = Career\ confidence$$

SKILLS – What are you good at? What do you have a knack for?

(Examples: writing, drawing, working with children, solving problems, building things, leading people, conceptualizing, bringing people together, organizing, singing, motivating others, planning, learning another language, gardening, dancing, fixing things)

Ask yourself some of the following questions for clues to uncovering your skills:

What do others say my skills are?

What do I enjoy doing because I know I can do it well?

What have previous employers noted on my reference letters?

What were my favourite activities as a child?

What am I complimented on?

What is something I do during which I lose track of time?

What do I find myself doing just because I enjoy it?

Summary of skills:

a

b

c

d

e

PASSIONS – What do you feel passionate about?

(Examples: food, family, working outdoors, faith, ideas, finding out how things work, art, fitness, teaching, friendships, travel, animals, helping others)

Ask yourself some of the following questions for clues to uncovering your passions:

What is important to me?

What kinds of TV programmes do I watch?

What kinds of magazines do I read?

What makes me angry?

What is something I can't imagine living without?

What holds my interest intensely?

What do I love?

What gives me energy?

What have I always been interested in?

What has always been a part of my life?

Summary of passions:

a

b

c

d

e

VALUES – What do you value most?

(Examples: family, faith, caring, security, trust, integrity, harmony, honesty, friends, loyalty, strength, creativity, freedom, hard work, support, bravery)

Ask yourself some of the following questions for clues to uncovering your values:

What do I value in some of my closest relationships?

What are my personal values?

What do I believe strongly in?

In what manner do I want to live my life?

Which values can I not imagine living my life without?

Which values improve my life?

Which values fulfil me?

What values do I want people to remember me having?

Summary of values:

a

b

c

d

e

LIFESTYLE – What would be your ideal lifestyle?

(Examples: home or flat, large or medium income, relationships with family, having a cottage on a lake, how many children, education, being your own boss, being admired by others, time to spend on hobbies, control over your finances, travelling regularly)

Ask yourself some of the following questions for clues to uncovering your lifestyle:

What do I enjoy about my current lifestyle?

When I was younger, how did I dream my life would be?

Think of someone whose lifestyle you admire – what exactly do you admire about it?

Picture a perfect day in your ideal life – what does your lifestyle look like?

Complete the sentence: my life would be close to perfect if....

Summary of lifestyle short-term:

a

b

c

d

e

Summary of lifestyle long-term:

a

b

c

d

e

ENVIRONMENT – In what kind of an environment do you work well?

(Examples: positive, creative, teamwork, room or open plan, structured/no structure, free to work at my own pace, a trusting boss, good colleagues, a place where I can be a leader, fast-paced, varied or changing challenges, quiet, a place where I can maintain long relationships with people, risk-taking, flexible hours, big company, small company)

Ask yourself some of the following questions for clues to uncovering your environment:

What does my ideal work environment look like?

In what environments have I been most productive?

What kind of physical space do I work well in?

What elements in my current company culture do I appreciate?

What is important to me in a job environment?

What kind of leader do I perform best with?

How would I like to change the environment of my current job?

Summary of environment:

a

b

c

d

e

After compiling and prioritizing these lists, use them to rate your current job and a past position as to how well your skills, values, etc. were met. Rate each category from 1 to 10 – '10' meaning the job met everything on your list, and '1' meaning the job did not meet any of the criteria on the list. Please indicate which of your skills, etc. you were able to utilize or express.

Take note of themes and trends within each of the categories. For example, imagine that one of your natural talents was for music. In each of your past positions that scored low, you might notice that you were unable to use your musical talents. You may determine that you value this talent in yourself, and should perhaps be looking for different ways to express it.

FIGURE 9.1   Your current job

Current Job Title:	
Skills:	Skills Criteria Met – rate on a scale of 1 to 10: • • •
Passions:	Passions Criteria Met – rate on a scale of 1 to 10: • • •
Values:	Values Criteria Met – rate on a scale of 1 to 10: • • •
Lifestyle:	Lifestyle Criteria Met – rate on a scale of 1 to 10: • • •
Environment:	Environment Criteria Met – rate on a scale of 1 to 10: • • •

What have you learned from this exercise? What information do you take away, both personally and in regards to your career? Act on what you have learned to make changes in your current job or start to look for pastures new.

Gretchen Ruben was a lawyer and happily married to the love of her life. Everything seemed settled. One day when in her friend's apartment she noticed large legal tomes piled up in her lounge. She asked if these were part of her course and her friend said, no she just enjoyed reading them. At that moment Gretchen realized that she only read what she had to for her work and no more. She had no love of the law. What she did rush home and do was write. Her passion was for writing, so after much soul-searching she became a

FIGURE 9.2 A previous job

Past Job Title:	
Skills:	**Skills Criteria Met – rate on a scale of 1 to 10:** • • •
Passions:	**Passions Criteria Met – rate on a scale of 1 to 10:** • • •
Values:	**Values Criteria Met – rate on a scale of 1 to 10:** • • •
Lifestyle:	**Lifestyle Criteria Met – rate on a scale of 1 to 10:** • • •
Environment:	**Environment Criteria Met – rate on a scale of 1 to 10:** • • •

writer. She strongly felt that enthusiasm for something is even more important than innate skill. She wrote *The Happiness Project* and it became a best-seller.

So let the insights gleaned from the last section guide you to what you love, value and have passion for most, and then plan. This change does not have to be instant and can be a spare time activity till you are ready to launch into a new business, career or promoted post.

Don't wait to be confident to go for promotion or a new post. Just do it because then you will become confident. Action precedes change. It is a good motto to remember.

Steps to confidence at work

- Work out what you want and don't want from work.
- Realize it's always more than the money.
- Use the career confidence formula.
- Remember action precedes change.

Chapter Ten
Knowing the words to the song

All the CEOs and recruiters I talked to about what they looked for in a colleague or new hire mentioned a passion for work and an ability to communicate details of that with evidence. One of our coaches, Karen Dunleavy, spoke about this recently when she described interviewing a young woman who was entirely credible on paper but when asked to document her experience could only talk in generalities, not her specific experience. Despite Karen's encouragement to reflect on past successes she had no words, no story. They then doubted her ability to deliver and so could not employ her.

Tom DiPuma spoke of first going on stage as a singer and completely drying up, not realizing that he had to take time to learn his words; do his preparation. He made sure after that he did his homework. For him, confidence is 'knowing the words to the song'. In a more symbolic way it means having a vocabulary that describes your contribution, your background experience, your natural skills and the benefits a business partner will get from associating with you.

'Your leadership style' is a quick version of a kind of Myers Briggs assessment that I have created. It only takes minutes to complete. There are three questions and it will lead to the discovery of how you lead. A coaching client who completed it last week commented that she now had a whole new language to use for convincing her boss that she should be promoted.

I put together this short version, as short always works for me, and it meant that I could really work out my unique contribution to my own team and no longer did I have to try to be anybody else. My preferred style suited me. I could exult in it, relax about my strengths, and be confident about my contribution. The other exciting result is that it allows you to hire a team of people different from you if you are a team leader. For me this is true diversity. At work it certainly shouldn't matter what colour you are, what sex, or sexual orientation; diversity is about contribution and this questionnaire identifies that.

So complete it with attention and score your results. Read the description pertaining to your type and then on page 85 – using the three letters of your key – work out your personal leadership style. Read the descriptions of your leadership style as this will provide you with that vocabulary you need to tell your story, to talk about your contribution. Continue on to perception, judgement and career interests. Again this shows the difference between your selected style and the others.

Why leadership style? Some of you may not be leaders yet or perhaps never want to be a leader of others, however this questionnaire can be associated with how you lead your expertise at work, your communications, how you go about collecting information or simply how you lead your life.

Your leadership style

Instructions

There are only three questions to answer, but you should give them serious thought to get the most out of this.

The whole process shouldn't take more than a few minutes. But for less than five minutes, you'll get more personality information about yourself than assessments that take five times as long!

There are three sets of dichotomies and you'll have to choose one over the other in each of the three. Remember we all have a little of each in our personalities... just choose the one that you feel more comfortable with most of the time.

The more carefully you consider each item, the more accurate the results will be. And no criticism that it's too hard to pick only one of the two choices – it's the nature of the beast. The pay-off will be worth it!

Q1 – These preferences have to do with how you collect information... or what you pay attention to.

column A	column B
• Learn new things by imitation and observation. • Value solid, recognizable methods achieved in step-by-step manner. • Focus on actual experience. • Tend to be specific and literal; give detailed descriptions. • Behave practically. • Rely on past experiences. • Like predictable relationships. • Appreciate standard ways to solve problems. • Methodical. • Value realism and common sense.	• Learn new things through general concepts. • Value different or unusual methods achieved via inspiration. • Focus on possibilities. • Tend to be general and figurative; use metaphors and analogies. • Behave imaginatively. • Rely on hunches. • Values change in relationships. • Use new and different ways to solve problems and reach solutions. • Do things in a roundabout way. • Value imagination and innovation.
Again, we all take in info in both ways. But one way is used more often. Try to think about which one you feel most comfortable with.	
Choice A ☐	**Choice B** ☐

Q2 – This category deals with how we make decisions and reach conclusions...

column A	column B
• Have truth as an objective. • Decide more with my head. • Question others' findings, 'cause they might be wrong. • Notice ineffective reasoning. • Choose truthfulness over tactfulness. • Deal with people firmly, as needed. • Expect the world to run on logical principles. • Notice pros and cons of each option. • See others' flaws... I am critical. • I believe feelings are valid if they're logical.	• Have harmony as a goal. • Decide more with my heart. • Agree more with others' findings, because people are worth listening to. • Notice when people need support. • Choose tactfulness over truthfulness. • Deal with people compassionately. • Expect the world to recognize individual differences. • Note how an option has value and it affects people. • Like to please others; show appreciation. • I believe any feeling is valid.
Which one jumps out at you as 'just feeling like you?'	
Choice A ☐	**Choice B** ☐

Q3 – The one has to do with the lifestyle you adopt.

column A	column B
• Prefer my life to be decisive, imposing my will on it.	• Seek to adapt my life and experience to what comes along.
• Prefer knowing what I'm getting myself into.	• Like adapting to new situations.
• Feel better after making decisions.	• Prefer to keep things open.
• Enjoy finishing things.	• Enjoy starting things.
• Work for a settled life, with my plans in order.	• Keep my life as flexible as possible so that nothing's missed.
• Dislike surprises and want advance warnings.	• Enjoy surprises and like adapting to last-minute changes.
• See time as a finite resource, and take deadlines seriously.	• See time as a renewable resource, and see deadlines as elastic.
• Like checking off a 'to do' list.	• Ignore a 'to do' lists, even if I have made one.
• Feel better with things planned.	• Would rather do whatever comes along.
• Like to be settled, organized.	• Tentative, flexible, spontaneous.
Again choose which one 'feels right'... like an old pair of shoes?	
Choice A ☐	**Choice B** ☐

Scoring

Please write your choice, A or B, for each of the three questions (eg Q1 – A, Q2 – B, Q3 – A).

In the grid below you will find 8 different combinations of A and B choices.

Q1	Q2	Q3

Match your choice to one on the grid below and obtain your key (eg if your choice is B-A-B, your KEY is NTP.

	choice	style
Q1	A	STJ
Q2	A	
Q3	A	

	choice	style
Q1	A	SFJ
Q2	B	
Q3	A	

	choice	style
Q1	B	NFJ
Q2	B	
Q3	A	

	choice	style
Q1	B	NTJ
Q2	A	
Q3	A	

	choice	style
Q1	A	STP
Q2	A	
Q3	B	

	choice	style
Q1	A	SFP
Q2	B	
Q3	B	

	choice	style
Q1	B	NFP
Q2	B	
Q3	B	

	choice	style
Q1	B	NTP
Q2	A	
Q3	B	

Your KEY is:

Two out of the three letters of your KEY, eg SJ from STJ or NF from NFP, lead to your leadership style. This is revealed in the table below and there are descriptions of each leadership style.

Leadership styles

NF – Diplomats	Search for unique identity and meaning. Value empathic, meaningful relationships. Generally enthusiastic. Want to make the world a better place. Trust their intuition and imagination. Think in terms of integration and similarities. Focus on developing potential in others, finding a purpose in life, and bridging differences. Want to be authentic.
NT – Strategists	Theory oriented. Seek to understand the principles on which the world and everything in it work. Trust logic and reason. Sceptical and precise. Think in terms of differences, categories, definitions and structures. Focus on strategies and designs that achieve long-range goals and lead to progress. Want competence and thorough knowledge.
SP – Tacticians	Action and impact oriented. Very practical, they hunger for spontaneity. Optimistic. Trust luck and ability to handle whatever comes up. Absorbed in the moment. Read people and situations and adapt to changes to get the job done. Seek adventure and experiences. Think in terms of variations. Focus on tactics to help others and get desired results. Want freedom to choose their next action.
SJ – Organizers	Hunger for responsibility and predictability. Like standard operating procedures to protect and preserve. Serious and concerned. Trust the past, tradition and authority. Think in terms of comparisons, sequences and associations. Focus on logistics to support people, maintain organisations and achieve objectives. Want security, stability and to belong.

The four leadership styles

Diplomats	Organizers
• Build bridges between people. • Have empathy. • Strive to unify by understanding and resolving deeper issues while honouring individual uniqueness. • Move to a level of abstraction to see how two seemingly different views are alike and then to choose a symbolic way of communicating the similarity. • Help others harmonize and clarify their values to bring unity to the individual and the group. • Have foresight and vision with implications for developing the people involved, then communicating that vision so it is accepted and followed. • Help others find their path and inspire them to follow it. • Mentor others to achieve the envisioned potential.	• Provide the logical support and protection necessary for people to get things done, make sure things go well. • Provide service and caretaking that help people get underway. • Get the right thing and the right information, in the right place, at the right time, to the right people. • Attend to people's comforts and make things easy for others. • Standardize, establish, and oversee policies and procedures that provide stability for the group. • Investigate what has happened before, carefully describing where we want to go and how to get there, and monitoring the plan along the way. • Shelter and protect to ensure safety and well-being. • Examine, assess and instruct to meet standards.
Strategists	**Tacticians**
• Think of and explain all the possible contingencies and influencing factors and then design processes for achieving the objectives. • Abstractly analyse a situation and consider previously unthought-of-possibilities. • Look at the relationship between the goals and the means. • Identify the ways and means to achieve a well defined goal. • Integrate ideas into cohesive theories and design processes that strategically meet the wants and needs of others. • Implement a vision of the future – conceiving of a way to be as well as the action steps needed to get there. • Generate and share a multitude of ideas and possibilities for action. • Mobilise and coordinate actions of others to implement a strategy.	• Read the current situation and skilfully manage the situation. • Effect a desired result, often coming up with a variety of solutions. • Take action according to the needs of the moment and plan the next move. • Cleverly display, compose and perform with attention to impact and effect. • Compose and produce just the right result that expresses the input of all those concerned. • Analyse and look at all the angles beforehand, getting a sense of the situation and then being free to operate in the moment as things change. • Motivate others, often though a lively and moving presentation. • Promote and execute actions in response to the varying demands of the situation, going around obstacles when necessary.

Perception, judgement and career interests

Preferred style	Organizers SJ	Tacticians SP	Diplomats NF	Strategists NT
Focus on:	Facts	Facts	Possibilities	Possibilities
Handle these by applying:	Objective analysis and experience	Personal warmth and concern for others	Attention to potential	Theoretical concepts and systems
Thus tend to become:	Practical and analytical	Sympathetic and friendly	Insightful and enthusiastic	Logical and analytical
Find scope for their interests in:	Technical skills with objects and facts	Practical help and services for people	Understanding and encouraging people	Theoretical and technical frameworks
For example:	Applied science Business Administration Banking Law enforcement Production Construction	Health care Community service Teaching Supervision Religious service Support services Sales	Psychology Human resources Teaching Research Literature Religious service Healthcare Art & music	Physical science Research Management Computers Law Engineering Technical work

I am a diplomat who is oriented towards people and harmonization. And yes, I am conceptual. I am often heard to say that I don't want to contaminate an argument with any detail. And diplomats are often psychologists. How accurate is that result!

My husband John is tactical – very practical and detail conscious. He is a chemical engineer, an environmentalist saving us all from nasty emissions and waste products. Actually, this questionnaire should be completed by your significant other before committing to a business partnership or marriage. At least you will know who you are getting into bed with – literally or metaphorically.

Strategists are also conceptual and like a theoretical underpinning but, in addition, they really like a plan. They are implementers or more likely they will delegate the implementing and enjoy coordinating the input. Marthinus, a coaching consultant with RTG, enjoys the vision of where we are going with the coaching school but always wants to see the plan. He is a strategist.

My PA is an organizer and I really need an organizer in my life. I gave her this questionnaire at interview, saw the results and gave her the job on the spot. It was a marriage made in heaven and she has been with me, woman and girl.

Remember, when I talk about being a leader I don't mean necessarily the ultimate leader or CEO but being a team leader, a head of department or leader of your own expertise. We are all leaders in one way or another.

This next exercise really identifies differences in style.

Think about how you would buy a car. You might of course be very 'green' and eschew car buying and driving anything. Humour me and write down how, if you were to buy a car, you would go about it:

-
-
-
-

Review your results.

Would you buy a car spontaneously, perhaps seeing one in a showroom and immediately rushing in to purchase? If so, you would definitely be a diplomat. You love a sleek looking vehicle with nice design and lines. You might be heard to say that a car is 'stroke-able'. I bought my car when a friend, meeting me at Edinburgh Airport, mentioned a car sale nearby. The salesman demonstrated how the hood went into the boot and the deal was done immediately. What was there not to like?

If you prefer speed and a bit of a roar from your engine at the traffic lights then you are more than likely a tactician. You will talk in terms of 'performance', engine size and nippiness at the traffic lights. During a Leadership Masterclass recently, three of the tacticians had received speeding tickets over the last three months.

Enjoying the process of researching your new car, using *Which* magazine and drawing up a checklist means you are a strategist.

Some strategists take up to a year to make up their minds on make and specification. I was using this exercise with a group of senior leaders in Shell recently and the group of strategists who were discussing how to buy a car were turning their eyes purposely to my flip chart. Eventually they asked if they could use it. Up went a checklist with tick boxes about the steps to buying a car.

Organizers often don't understand the question. They are heard to ask, 'Why wouldn't you buy the same car you have always bought? If it worked before, why not now?'

They are more likely to think about the logistics of golf bags in the boot, child seats in the back. A few green issues appear in this group too; petrol consumption, electric plug-in efforts and exhaust fumes. All things utterly alien to diplomats, who are stroking their cars. Diplomats will look at organizers and strategists as if from another planet with their research, checklists and logistics. They are more likely to understand a fast tactician.

So it is a case of *Vive la difference*! We need all styles to complete a team at work. It is diversity that helps us see another point of view so that our product or service can reach a variety of markets. Become conversant with the language of your style, read your descriptions till the words change to become your words and you can use them internally, ready for use externally when called upon.

What confidence that questionnaire inspires as everyone can exult in who they are but also get people around them to support their downsides and weaknesses. This is exhilarating stuff.

Telling your story

Understanding your skills, passions, values, etc. and also your leadership style, you are ready to tell your story; how you gained your expertise, what you now want to do and where you want to go. Stories are not generalities. They have beginnings and endings with people involvement. It is amazing to me that these simple rules are forgotten. Stories should also be concise, so concentrate on highlights.

Here are a couple of examples:

STORY 1

My husband was a lab assistant, working at BP when he left school. He realized that to the other assistants the job meant a salary and not much else. They rushed home at night to play golf or football and that was the summit of their lives, which was fine for them but not him. He found himself saying, 'There must be more than this'. Encouraged (browbeaten) by his mother, he attended night classes that led him to study chemical engineering at university. He did return to BP but as an environmental engineer. His attention to detail and ability to present his ideas well as a tactician led to career success. He is passionate about the subject, has had a wonderful career and still travels the world saving us all from nasty emissions and the toxicity of waste products. Because he feels that his talents are being put to good use, he has confidence in his expertise.

STORY 2

Tom DiPuma started his IT career with IBM, which he always says was a great foundation for learning. He and a partner then founded a company that financed the brokerage and leasing of high-end computers. Having the contacts and knowledge to find, solicit and execute the transactions was unique at the time. The business was very competitive, but the experience led to strong and long-lasting relationships. Tom is a strategist; he has a clear vision of where he is going and the skills to implement that vision. This became slightly derailed, however, after losing a $1.2 million deal and his planned $150K commission. Tom was bemoaning this fact to his airline seat-mate on the way home from a business trip. The seat-mate pointed out that he was very lucky that he had a job that could lose him $150K in one day (or make it). It changed his view of his working life. He saw himself as the successful person he was.

Steps to confidence at work

- Understand your leadership style, no matter what kind of leader you are.

- Learn the language of your preferred style.

- If selling yourself at interview, while networking, or going for promotion, use the descriptions of your leadership style to position your uniqueness.

- *Vive la différence* – this is true diversity.

- Tell your story with confidence about how you have got to where you are now.

Chapter Eleven
The user-friendly confident you

Throughout this branding process you have to ask yourself 'what's in it for them?' for employers to want to hire, partner or act as an advocate for you. This WIIFT factor is paramount when considering what you offer. In other words, you have to think about the benefits of you. You may have decided, having read so far, that you should change to be a more 'user-friendly' person in order to be more successful, but how can you do that?

My ITEA process guarantees change if you follow the four important quadrants below.

FIGURE 11.1 Four quadrants for change

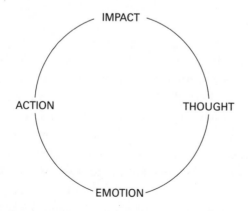

Impact

What impact do you have on others? I am thinking of Oli Norman's 'mood hoovers'. Do people feel good till they meet you? Consistent negativity is a turn-off and the antithesis of a confident demeanour. CEOs and recruiters talk about energy, a light in the eye, open body language. These all comprise impact. There is an instinctive drawing to or repelling away from some people. We call it 'gut reaction' but this reaction is actually a long way from the gut; it is in the brain – the amygdala to be specific. Psychologists argue about the timing but we have an instant subcortical response followed by a signal from the amygdala to the prefrontal cortex which becomes a thought. Regardless of the physical manifestations, I am sure you would agree that an impact that draws people towards you rather than repelling them is devoutly to be wished.

The ingredients of a good impact are smiling, direct eye contact, firm handshake and relaxation. This creates the impact of energy, something given rather than subtracted. Anxiety, on the other hand, is contagious and sets the person who receives your negative impact on edge. It takes about five seconds to create an adverse impact and thirty seconds to make an appealing one. First impressions are paramount in business. In our instant, frenzied world, it might be your only opportunity.

Thought

It is challenging to change your thinking style but realizing that you are in charge of your thoughts is a start. The mantra approach can work. Create a short phrase that makes sense to you. Mine was 'I'm OK', and I have often used 'I will cope as I always do' when crises occur. Moving up an organization and bringing others into your team can be a testing time for your confidence. The best leaders choose people who are more skilled than they are. We have all heard that. But what it means is that you have to be so secure in your thinking about yourself that you can openly reward your staff.

Many people in senior positions do not have sufficient self-esteem to deliver that. So thinking that you are OK and others are too is a start. Your thoughts then give rise to emotions. Understandably if your thoughts are positive, optimistic and solution-focused then your feelings are more likely to be of the positive variety too.

Emotion

I cannot imagine you have not all heard of emotional intelligence but having knowledge and being skilled emotionally are two different things. We all experience feelings but strong or uncomfortable ones are those we shy away from expressing or over-express when pushed. Having a vocabulary that describes our emotions as we experience them, in a calm and focused way, is true emotional intelligence. Of course that calm expression is at the very heart of confidence, especially at work where unbridled emotional expression can be frowned on.

Handling challenging people elegantly fits into this quadrant as well as being able to give and receive critical feedback.

Action

And of course, all of the above are useless unless you change your behaviour. The behaviour we are talking about here is for business networking, interviews for promotion or any meeting where you want to impress. It is often difficult to guess at someone's thinking style or how they handle their feelings but you can judge their behaviour.

The skills and behaviour that flow from being emotionally in touch are what the majority of the CEOs and recruiters are talking about in this chapter; openness and honesty with the people around you, rewarding eight times more than you criticize, handling difficult people with elegance, supplying critical feedback to enhance rather than damage. No one wants to hire someone, especially in the boardroom, who is going to be intransigent, no matter how right they are. There is a huge difference between disagreeing or being critical about a project and being difficult. The first can be skilled, the latter unskilled. You must consider all four ingredients as a package for change.

I remember a Maths teacher who was very good at his job but promotion to head teacher eluded him despite many interviews. The students in his classes were inspired by him, many going on to University to study the subject. However he had very strong views about the education system and its treatment of Mathematics as a subject. He aired these opinions at interview. Nothing at all wrong with that but it was the way he delivered the message. He made it personal, naming people in authority, using epithets to describe them. He was a volcano of anger and righteous indignation and a bit scary in behaviour. I had to coach him to consider the impact he was making, helped him to relax and deliver the same message but talking about his feelings rather than acting them out. We then practised the interview using video feedback so that he could see how he came across and his behaviour changed. Following the next interview he was promoted and was then in a more powerful position to change things in the direction he desired.

Great influencing skills are outlined in Part Three. All of these are of paramount importance to confidence at work. So if you need to change, read the next chapters for further insights and skills for confidence.

Branding you

Companies have nurtured their brand through all the details of the customer experience. A brand map exists in all of our minds. If I say toothpaste, you think ___. If I say fizzy drink, you think ___. If I say fashion, you think ___. If I say furniture, you think ___.

A brand is great at a particular set of things. Once brands are established, they are very powerful and yet very fragile, especially in a globally connected economy. Remember Gerard Ratner. Also Toyota had to recall vehicles because of mechanical problems; their expenditure on television advertising to reinforce their commitment to quality during that time would have rivalled the GNP of a small country for a year. They were extremely worried that their brand had been tarnished.

So a question for you is, 'what is your brand?' Are you a nippy Mini or a shiny Mercedes? Both are very useful in their own way, but completely different. What professional attributes are you consistently known for? Are you known as a terrific troubleshooter or a strategist? What kind of problems are you consistently drawn to? Is there a particular expertise that you are known for? What kind of meetings are you asked to join and why? What are you NOT known for?

Why is branding important from a career perspective? Well, it creates and draws new opportunities to you. Remember, branding is the attributes that people are drawn to or pushed away from. Are people drawn to you? What for, and what do they ask for? Look at these examples of branded products:

- BMW: competitive achievement.
- Chrysler: cars that dare to stand out.
- Coca-Cola: refreshing the mind, body and spirit.
- Federal Express: guaranteed, delivery on time.
- Mercedes: technical innovation.
- Virgin: more fun, more value.

I have had the honour of developing senior scientists to become even more senior with aspirations to the boardroom. Some of my courses were focused on women. So often their brand was motherly. They would socialize with secretaries and lab staff and therefore the perception of them was domestic. The brand was not that of a leading-edge leader in corporate life. Wearing long skirts and bringing baked cookies in for coffee break did not work for their promotion prospects to the higher echelons.

Now before you shout 'sexist' at me, let me explain. There is nothing wrong with any of these domestic niceties but they are not part of a corporate leader's repertoire. If of course you start your own company, bake away! You are the boss.

So your brand has to suit your aspirations. Once you are team leader, head of department or even CEO, roll on the cookie competitions.

Personal brands can be just as easily damaged as those of products or companies. Some brand damaging circumstances might be:

- Getting drunk at the office party.
- Wearing something inappropriate to work – torn jeans, an unwashed shirt, a low cut blouse, too short a skirt.
- Losing your temper at a board meeting.
- Not preparing for a presentation.
- Taking personal credit when the team does well and blaming them when things go badly.
- Not keeping confidences.
- Constant negativity.

Consistency of brand is important if you are changing to become more user-friendly for example. Perhaps try saying 'good morning' in a lively way or 'well done' for some special input. You have to persist with the new behaviour for three weeks to get rid of the old grumpy bad habits and another nine weeks for that new behaviour to becomea new habit.

Now have fun with the 'one minute branding' workout below. Complete the questions fairly quickly and spontaneously. When completed, put together a branding statement that encapsulates the spirit of your answers. Then create a slogan that defines your brand. This should be short and pithy and easily remembered. I am giving you an example of the Bob Clyde brand. Bob is one of our coaches and a long-standing friend. My husband, who was looking over my shoulder as I was writing this part of the chapter, saw the list but without a name attached. He immediately said, 'oh that's Bob isn't it?' So your list of attributes can really reflect who you are.

The one-minute branding workout

FIGURE 11.2   The one-minute branding workout

Brand personality traits	Answer	Reasons for answer
If you were a car what would that be?		
If you were a colour what would that be?		
If you were an item of confectionery what would that be?		
If you were a drink what would that be?		
If you were a fashion label what would that be?		
If you were a retail outlet, what would that be?		

Your personal branding statement and slogan

Statement:

Slogan:

FIGURE 11.3   The Bob Clyde brand

Bob Clyde, Executive Coach

Brand personality traits	Answer	Reasons for answer
If you were a car what would that be?	Mercedes 230–4 door diesel	Quality of construction, reliability and prestige
If you were a colour what would that be?	Rich royal blue	Has associations of comfort, warmth, cosiness, night
If you were an item of confectionery what would that be?	Soft centred chocolate	A wee bit hard on the outside but soft in the middle
If you were a drink what would that be?	A glass of red wine	Associated with conviviality and close friends
If you were a fashion label what would that be?	Marks and Spencer	Value for money, no nonsense and you can take things back
If you were a retail outlet, what retail outlet would that be?	The butchers shop in Blackheath	Personal attention, better quality of meat, would go out of my way to go to it

Bob's personal branding statement and slogan

Statement: The reliability of a Mercedes, the old world charm and values of the family run shop, throw in a glass of the warm south, preferably French red, with a side dish of no-nonsense value for money M&S, and you have a picture of a man who never drinks and drives, doesn't mind being seen in his eco-friendly royal blue diesel Merc filled with friends and wearing a M&S pullover.

Slogan: Values of the past that look to the future.

With your personal brand you are now ready to greet your public with the confidence born of knowing who you are and what you can contribute to work. Use your brand slogan when you meet people at events, when you go for interview, even on your business cards.

Steps to confidence at work

- After reading the comments from CEOs and recruiters, if necessary change yourself to become more user-friendly with the analysis of your impact, thinking style, emotional intelligence and actions.

- Create your brand using the one minute branding workout.

- Use your brand statement whenever possible to instil confidence.

Part Three
Influencing for confidence at work

Overview

Confidence does not exist in isolation. You have to interact with others and the nature of this interaction becomes a major underpinning for confidence at work. Good influencing skills achieve buy-in from those around you and woo people to your point of view. Now that authoritarianism has been shown to demotivate people at work, the skills of influence have taken centre stage.

There are ten major principles of influencing. I started on a path of discovering these principles by taking part in the BBC programme *Scambusters*. I had to analyse a number of videotapes of nasty people who carried out scams on the most vulnerable in society, the elderly, the disabled and those in pain. Those scammers were thoroughly disreputable but what began to occur to me was that as professional swindlers they were very skilled in influencing techniques. They had spent much time and trouble honing their presentations for maximum effect and I wondered whether the same amount of time was spent by good, well-intentioned people who wanted to influence for splendid causes. I thought possibly not.

So here are the top ten principles that I extracted from these videos so that you as a good, well-intentioned reader can use them to get what you want.

1 Likeability

2 Similarity

3 Knee-jerk thinking

4 Reward

5 Reciprocity

6 Edification

7 W.I.I.F.T.

8 Elegance when handling challenging people

9 Perseverance

10 Enthusiasm

All of these skills can be put to good use especially when networking. In fact I would say that you cannot network effectively without good influencing skills. Networking has been shown to be of major importance for those desiring promotion or pastures new at work. So defining your existing networks as well as exploring new ones and utilizing your influencing skills to network, will conclude this chapter.

The principles of influencing and the skills for networking add another layer of expertise to increase confidence at work.

Chapter Twelve
Likeability and similarity

Likeability is top of the list as an influencing factor. Defence lawyers work with their clients to make them likeable to a jury as there is much evidence to show that the likeability factor will make the difference between a verdict of guilty and of innocent. Even surgeons, who have cut off the wrong body part, will be excused and not sued if they are liked by their patient. Being liked is powerful.

The first thing I noticed was that these con men and women (a few were women) worked very hard to be likeable. They were well groomed, smiled a lot and had good interpersonal skills. Charming is the right word for them. The smiling thief is the one that takes us by surprise. My husband and I recently had lunch at a favourite restaurant in Borough Market. Tables outside were hard to come by, so we shared one with a delightful couple. We exchanged holiday anecdotes, talked about where we both lived and how they both worked in the City. I do remember them asking if we had received their bill by mistake. We hadn't. They left, we thought, to pay their bill at the desk inside, when in fact they simply left leaving us to pay for them. We were nonplussed, as they seemed extremely pleasant. Their routine was flawless and I am sure we have not been the only ones to be left paying their bills.

Of course I am not suggesting you do anything like that but simply understand that the likeability factor is so powerful. Salespeople go on many training courses so that they can use this factor to sell you things that you probably don't want. When we are in liking mode, we are compliant. When we feel dislike, we are propelled in the other direction.

I was invited to speak for a large accountancy firm at a conference in Switzerland. The entire consultancy group with directors, associates and administrators were accommodated in splendid hotels for two days and took over all the restaurants in town for dinner in the evening. This was an expensive trip.

The dinner table I was at was hosted by one of the directors. He was talking to another director about skiing down some blue run and then going off-piste as it hadn't been challenging enough. The conversation was competitive and macho. Seated either side of him were two young female secretaries. He turned to them and asked where they had skied. Excitedly, they both replied they had tried snowboarding. A long pause, then he resumed the conversation across the table with his male colleague, ignoring the young women for the rest of the evening.

I noticed the looks on the faces of the two secretaries. Dislike and disgust. The next morning at breakfast, I joined the admin group table. Perhaps this lack of interpersonal nous I had seen from the director was an isolated instance. Sadly not. I overheard one administrator saying, 'Well we kind of thought the directors were idiots, now we know they are'.

Fancy going to all that expense to make things worse. The concept of taking the whole consultancy group away had been a wonderful one but these directors had no idea how to make themselves likeable to young people outside their ambit and possessed no skills to make connections.

What the director could have done was to ask open-ended questions about snowboarding. It may not have been his 'thing' but he could have shown interest. Questions such as: 'How did it feel to snowboard?', 'How challenging was it?', 'Where did you go?', 'How was it in comparison to skiing?' Any or all of these responses would have worked. Asking questions shows interest and makes the person you are talking to feel important. How different would have been the breakfast conversation with administration staff the following morning if the directors had just been interested enough to ask questions and listen.

Of course there needs to be some interested and likeable body language attached to this questioning behaviour. By turning his back on the young women he was talking to, his behaviour was entirely the opposite of likeable. What he could have done was lean forward and smile. See below for a list of likeable, and therefore influencing, body language.

Influencing body language and its meaning

smiling	happy, confident, at ease
direct gaze	nothing to hide
head erect	confident in relationships
good posture	high self-esteem
open gestures	open, honest person
head to one side	listening positively
leaning forward	interested in what is being said
nodding	approval of another person's point of view

Similarity

A friend who is a psychiatrist of note, Dr Julian Bird, commented after being an examiner for young graduates for medical posts, that one of them had been impressive because of his ability to become a chameleon with his patients. He could change to suit the person in front of him without losing who he was or being patronizing in any way. Julian commented that he wished he could bottle that ability or indeed tease out the components to train others to have it. Not only is that a great therapeutic skill but successful for influencing skills.

So this next principle is that of similarity. We are strongly influenced by 'people like us'. The unprincipled influencers I saw on video would spend a lot of time looking at photographs on mantelpieces seeking out areas of similarity then talking about holidays in similar places, children or grandchildren of similar ages. The clothes they wore were those that an older generation would think of as 'proper'.

Mirroring

Many salespeople are now trained in body language and the concept of mirroring. Mirroring involves taking up the same body language as the person you are with so that they will feel at one with what you are saying. Knowing these techniques will help you in two ways. You can resist a salesperson when you don't want to buy something and use the techniques to relax someone you want to listen to you.

When I started in business and was hiring colleagues to work with me, I chose people I thought would bond into a cohesive team. Six months later one left, three months after that another. They left to start their own businesses. When the third left I knew something was very wrong. Were they seeing me setting up in business and thinking, 'well if she can do it so can we?' I was happy for them that they had their own ideas and were pursuing them, but where was I going wrong with my selection? It was the similarity principle. I was hiring people like me; potential entrepreneurs, who had business ideas, were initiators and self-starters. I then used the personal styles questionnaire you completed in Chapter 10 and never made that mistake again. I need people different from me to back up my deficiencies.

Boardrooms are filled with 'people like us', which is why diversity has such a hard time getting traction. When money is at stake, those at the top do not want to take undue risks and 'people not like us' are a risk. No matter how much research demonstrates that a diverse boardroom is a more successful one, similarity rules. Norway had to mandate that at least 40 per cent of board appointments should be women before fear of the law overcame the power of the similarity factor. Only now Norway is reaching parity of the sexes in the boardroom.

Equality

Women, different racial groups or gender orientations are unknown quantities and strike fear into hearts. When I interviewed 80 successful chief executives for my book *Fast Track to the Top*, of the 60 men I interviewed, only two had working wives. They may have worked before their marriage but certainly didn't after. So for these top men, working women were an unknown quantity.

A female banker friend of mine had to go to bars and strip clubs with the guys in the City as to refuse would make her too different and stop promotion prospects stone dead. She finally left when her boss put his expenses for prostitutes on her credit card. Enough was enough. She could never be like them.

So similarity is a powerful influencer and of course the more you network the more people you meet and the more diversity you can embrace. Great for confidence, great for business.

The skills of similarity are those of asking questions and finding out what you might have in common with the person you are meeting.

CASE STUDY

I still remain surprised by how people can look so confident but be lacking in confidence internally. I have also discovered that people can also be wildly confident in certain areas of their life and quivering jellies in others. *Psychologies* magazine asked me to meet a woman called Susan and help her with her lack of social confidence. I had an afternoon to make the desired change. We met for coffee, with Susan looking supremely confident in a corner of the café. Would anyone have guessed at my mission to increase her social confidence? I hardly think so.

Susan worked as a fund-raiser for a charity and in her office was fearless in pursuit of sponsorship and donations. However, when it came to socializing with work colleagues, she felt like the constant outsider. She told me that she had no idea how to approach people and not a clue what to say to them. In the office, with her own team, she felt totally in control of every interaction and confident, but outside, socializing with clients, she was quite the reverse. Two areas gave her particular concern: dinner parties with clients and large social events at conferences and fund-raisers.

Looking into her past she realized that both her father and her sister were shy and she thought she may have adopted their style of interaction. I reassured her that these skills, despite genetic inheritance, are learnt, just like those of driving a car.

She felt very strongly that clients and other business people would not be interested in anything she had to say outside the specific work arena. And she was not sure if they really would have anything in common – no similarity in other words. For the most part, she knew her clients enjoyed different pursuits to her, for example they loved football whereas she enjoyed visiting the latest exhibition at the National Gallery. I noticed that when she talked about art she was enthusiastic and animated, all lack of confidence gone. Football didn't get quite the same response. She was taciturn and negative.

She also had a firmly held belief that she had to talk a lot and sparkle in every social situation or she would have failed. Pretty exhausting and pressurizing.

I asked her how she might feel if she were in control of her social interactions and did not have the pressure to talk and sparkle at every turn. 'Released' was the word she used in reply. So below is what I suggested she might do to become socially confident and much more influential in a social setting around her business associates.

Susan had two invitations to business events following our meeting, so her challenge was to talk to at least six people at each event. This was the e-mail she sent me afterwards.

Well, what a week I've had!

Friday evening after the conference, I spoke to everyone using FORE and even managed some sort of conversation with some kids who were there with their parents (a bit of a breakthrough). It was useful that one of the most gregarious and vocal of this particular group wasn't there so I could get a word in edgeways, but none the less, I believe I would have held my own.

Tuesday evening – out for a meal with some sponsors and I think I did alright. I discovered that we had so much in common and we did not have to talk about football at all. They e-mailed me this morning to say thanks for a lovely evening, so that's grand. And I have been invited back to their office for another meeting followed by dinner.

So far, so good. I am determined to make a concerted effort to keep it up and develop this now. Fingers crossed I can as I feel so much more confident.

You certainly seem to have set me off on the right foot, so very many thanks for your help and advice – I am very grateful.

To be considered a great conversationalist, you may think you have to indulge in permanently witty repartee. Not so. The best way to initiate debate and conversation is to ask questions. It takes the spotlight away from you and onto the other person. What you are in fact doing is finding commonalities, similarities; things you might have in common, not differences like football versus art galleries.

When you ask your questions, remember FORE:

F = FAMILY

O = OCCUPATION

R = RECREATION

E = EDUCATION

These four areas of questioning work because they represent commonalities. We have all come from somewhere, had some kind of work at some point, had a hobby or pursuit, even if it was in the past, and we have all had to be educated. Of course you do not have to ask them in that order. Start with recreation if you are at the opening of the new fitness club or education when at the school reunion. Frankly the content of the questions hardly matters, it is the connection you make that counts, the looking for similarity.

Treat your next business/social encounter as an experiment. Move around the room talking to as many interesting people as you can using FORE in the time available, always looking for things in common-similarity. Be prepared to move on if someone starts to bore you or conversation flags. Thank them for the chat, smile and move.

I was running a Masterclass in leadership for the construction industry and, as was my wont, asked all the participants when they introduced themselves to talk about one thing they normally wouldn't divulge at first meeting. We had solicitors who were bikers in leathers in their spare time, kite fliers and pole dancers. What interesting revelations! When it came to the last two participants, the penultimate woman declared that she loved collecting driftwood and had a home full of 'natural sculptures' which her husband called kindling and kept trying to throw out. The woman next to her turned in shock saying, 'So do I. Every weekend I am on the beach looking for driftwood too'. They bonded and have met every week since that Masterclass. 'People like us' especially when they are 'unusual people like us' is a powerful influencer and relationship former.

Steps to confidence at work

- Use open-ended questions such as where, what, why, when and how to show interest and engender likeability.

- Alongside the questioning add some likeable body language of smiling, looking directly and leaning forward.

- Be aware of the power of the 'people like us' principle of similarity and use FORE to discover things you have in common with others.

- Be experimental. Try out these skills at your next business event and see what happens.

Chapter Thirteen
Knee-jerk thinking, reward and reciprocity

Knee-jerk thinking

There are some instant thinking patterns that influence our behaviour. I call it knee-jerk thinking. For the most part this is thinking we have been brought up with. One example might be, expensive = good.

The professor of psychology for my postgraduate degree was complaining that he had just too many private patients and he was worried that this would affect his university work with students. He was widely known as a neuropsychologist who assessed and rehabilitated people suffering from brain damage. He came up with a solution. He would double the cost of his sessions. This, in turn, unfortunately doubled his waiting list, so no solution there then. The last I heard he was starting an institute that would offer rehabilitation to all. Expensive = good.

Another knee-jerk thought is discount = bargain. Being Scottish, I am aware of the maxim that the Scots are mean. Of course, we are not mean at all, we just like value for money. So for many of us who come from backgrounds that were not replete with money, discount = bargain. My mother was an inveterate bargain hunter and even if a dress or piece of pottery was not on sale she would find some kind of flaw in it and would ask for a discount. Even now I find it difficult not to pass a discount rail in a fashion store, even if I have absolutely no need of anything to add to an already overcrowded wardrobe. The draw is there, the instant influence.

The scammers in the video made full use of this instant mechanistic thinking when they started with high prices for their reclining, back massaging chair, their special showers or their orthopaedic beds. They started with the expensive = good knee-jerk. They then gradually reduced the price with special offers if the purchase was made that day. Remember these people have gone to their targets' homes sometimes with an appointment, sometimes just arriving on their doorstep. It was, of course, an offer that would disappear when they did. So they very quickly followed up with the next knee-jerk, discount = bargain. And of course some people buy. If they want the goods, that is fine and if the goods are fine, that is fine too. But mostly they are not. The principle remains, however.

So how can you utilize this principle to good effect? When you are persuading a boss of your idea, impressing an interviewing panel with your candidacy for a job, confronting a team with a programme of change, then use language that will generate knee-jerk thinking. Today, that might be about savings to be made, increased revenue, or return on investment. For a team to be influenced about a change programme then security of employment might just do the trick.

Think about what would engender knee-jerk thinking in your audience, whoever that might be. Another concept here is that to communicate well and apply influence you must think like a listener. What rings your bell is not necessarily another's music.

I was working with a group of offshore medics in an oil company. They had tried for two years to implement an employee assistance programme (EAP) throughout the company. An EAP is a counselling service where staff can talk confidentially about any problem they have and these medics felt that it would create a 'feel good' factor. They also saw it as a good inducement for HR to use when recruiting. All of this fell on deaf ears. So what was important to this board of directors, I asked them? Savings, revenue, return on investment they replied! Their proposal was rejigged showing the return on investment of an EAP, the savings of cutting sickness absence and the increased revenue of more motivated people at their desks. It took a day for the proposal to be accepted.

So choosing language for good effect will motivate your listener to buy whatever you have to sell, and this is purposeful influencing.

Reward

Another huge influencer is reward. Psychologists learned this early on as a result of animal experiments. You could shock, speak sternly to or even, heaven forfend, hit a small furry animal but it would not move an inch towards a goal. Quite the reverse, it would freeze. The piece of cheese at the goalmouth, however, works a treat. Humans are not dissimilar. Whether we want to admit it or not we all like to be rewarded and not just with money, though that helps. Praise and encouragement are as important to us as the air we breathe.

My unprincipled influencers on video used reward to great effect. They would compliment the homeowner on the decor of the house, on pictures, photographs, anything so they could engender a positive feeling. These were lonely people who possibly had not experienced a positive comment for a long time. It upsets me even to write about this. Of course it leads to effective influence. If only good people with good causes would use this principle more often.

In his theory of 'transactional analysis', Eric Berne describes reward as stroking. Early behavioural experiments with monkeys revealed that if reared separately from their mothers, monkeys appeared comforted by a cloth substitute over a wire shape. They would rub up against it and hug it. If this was replaced by the wire 'monkey', without a cloth cover, the monkey did not touch it and became withdrawn.

The implications for human behaviour are plentiful. From birth we need to be hugged and stroked, not only to provide us with a sense of security and well-being but also to give us an awareness of the boundaries of our bodies. As we grow older, hugs and strokes are confined to intimate relationships but we still desire metaphorical stroking socially and at work. Just like the motherless monkey with the wire replacement, if these 'strokes' are absent then the result is behavioural withdrawal and attention-seeking.

Giving feedback in the workplace to colleagues and staff is essential to help them feel comfortable with what they are doing or to help them change. At its most fundamental, stroking is a greeting in the morning or a smile in passing. Deprivation of these social strokes leads to an uncaring attitude and a psychopathic organization.

Negative strokes are ways of diminishing people. Ignoring or 'putting down' others' ideas or contributions are common examples. Negative strokes are not to be confused with criticism which can be very positive and helpful if delivered in a friendly and self-developing way. Negative strokes discount people. They help to make them feel inadequate. They erode self-confidence and lead to resentment and overcautious behaviour.

Some examples of negative strokes are:

- being late;
- not consulting or involving people in decisions that affect them;
- asking for suggestions when you're already clear on your decision;
- hurrying people up rather than listening to them;
- closing an issue at a meeting before everyone feels heard;
- being condescending;
- refusing to acknowledge someone's expressed feelings;
- using jargon.

For example, saying to a colleague 'Call that a report?' instead of saying 'The introduction was good but you lost the argument in the middle', is a put-down with no detail given to enable change. This is the essence of negative stroking. Criticizing with helpful feedback as to how to improve is positive stroking, especially if balanced with what was good about the report.

When people discount themselves, for example, 'I don't know much about this, but...', they have probably been exposed to negative strokes. They no longer feel 'safe' and have stopped being clear, direct and open. This is the absolute opposite of confidence.

Some organizations are prone to blaming and negative stroking, none more than our political institutions and the media. Witch-hunts are commonplace and newspapers survive on the latest slurs. And yet we know that reward works. I asked a journalist once about this negativity. Exposure and blame he said were true, strong journalistic tactics, whereas that other 'nice' stuff was limp and sissy.

Rewards and stroking need not be expensive. A thank you, a card, a handshake, or even just a smile is all it takes. Sometimes rewards are conditional after completing a task, sometimes unconditional, simply for being there when you are with a loved one. Here are the rules for rewards.

Rewards should be:

- intermittent;
- specific;
- contingent;
- consistent;
- genuine;
- small;
- 8 to 1.

Intermittent. Strokes should be given sporadically, not every day or every week on a Friday. If they are repetitive they become like wallpaper and lose their effect. It is why 'person of the month' awards are not influencers of behaviour except to irritate those who did not get one.

Specific. If given for completing a project, task or report etc., then the one stroking should be very specific as to why the reward is being given. This increases the chances of the behaviour happening again.

Contingent. A stroke should happen as soon as the good behaviour is noticed. Any later and the power of the stroke is lost as the behaviour is forgotten.

Consistent. If you reward one person in the team then be sure to reward the next person who delivers the same. If not, then charges of unfairness will undermine all your positive efforts.

Genuine. A reward should always be genuinely meant, not because you feel you have to do it.

Small. Little tokens of reward, delivered intermittently, are better at influencing than big ones that are rare.

The 8 to 1 rule. If you reward four times more that you criticize then the performance of a team member, colleague, boss, child, or spouse will remain about the same. If you increase that to eight times then performance improvement is incremental. This result was gained as early as the 1970s from research with tutors and students at an American University.

Stroking can also work at the level of chat. I call it conversational cement. You know how, when you are talking to a work colleague about your holiday of a lifetime in California, and before you have put a period at the end of your sentence the person you are talking to has started describing their holiday, which you realize has to be longer, more expensive and better than yours. What they are revealing is an absence of conversational cement.

Always reward another's input with 'how interesting' or 'that sounds exciting' before moving on to your observations. It encourages a free exchange of views and opens people up to you.

A lack of conversational cement is usually a sign of lack of confidence. The confident allow others to have exciting experiences without having to compete. They are relaxed about you having the stage. When you meet new work colleagues, especially new bosses, if they have no conversational cement then they probably have poor delegation skills as they want the limelight for themselves. Check it out before joining that team.

A rewarding person, who uses strokes on a regular basis, will be a great influencer. Become that person and reap the rewards yourself.

Reciprocity

This brings us neatly on to the fifth principle, that of reciprocity. The *Scambusters* videos showed these salespeople turning up to their appointments with biscuits or some other kind of small gift. The concept of this is that when we receive a gift we feel obligated to return the favour.

When a sliver of cheese is given away at a cheese counter then customers generally buy the cheese. They may of course just like the taste but the principle of reciprocity is alive and working here. In fact there is the story of an Indiana supermarket that put out a whole cheese and let the customers cut off a piece. They sold an unprecedented 1,000 pounds of cheese in a few hours.

The Amway Corporation found that giving free samples to potential customers increased their turnover tenfold. Customers were given some cleaning fluid to try and when the salesperson went to collect it they found that most people bought the product. The power of reciprocity.

The social purpose of the reciprocity principle is to foster a mutual relationship so that a giver should not become a loser. There is a moving story of a German soldier who crossed no-man's-land in World War 1 to capture enemy soldiers for interrogation. He discovered an enemy soldier in a trench while he was eating and overpowered him easily. The enemy soldier offered him a piece of the bread he was eating and the German could neither kill him nor take him captive.

Perhaps today we are more sophisticated and know more about sales techniques but the networking organizations I talked about before work on the principle of reciprocity. If we like what they have to offer then it is a fine principle indeed. If not, then avoid.

If you want a reciprocal relationship, one that helps another and also helps you, then find a way to give them something. It may not have to be a free gift but could be a contact or help of some kind. This help may not be reciprocated by that individual but a giving philosophy, I firmly believe, will be rewarded in the long term. They may tell someone else and that of course creates word of mouth.

Of course it is related to what we spoke about in Chapter 1; that when we orientate ourselves towards others then we become more confident. The influencing principle of reciprocity falls into this category. Through helping others you can help yourself towards greater confidence. This is an especially important influencing principle when networking.

Steps to confidence at work

- When you want to influence an individual or group, work out in advance what words will have a knee-jerk response getting them saying yes to what you have to offer.

- Become a rewarding person who genuinely uses positive strokes.

- Remember the 8 to 1 rule.

- Incorporate conversational cement when talking to colleagues in order to create rewarding and influential relationships.

- Understand the power of reciprocity. You have to give to get. Networking relies on this principle of giving contacts and help to those you meet.

Chapter Fourteen
Handling challenging people with elegance

Knowing that you can handle any difficult person or situation is a major aspect of confidence. For my clients it is often the most compelling skill in their confidence armoury.

Colleagues at work can have a myriad of reasons to be challenging but I believe that challenge means that they care and are at least motivated to be difficult. If you can turn around this person by listening to their problems, then you will have a loyal member of staff.

Of course you may not be successful in all cases and occasionally you are left having to influence a member of your team directly to change their behaviour. The following script called the DESC script is perfect for providing feedback. I have written extensively about this but it remains one of the most used skills in my coaching armoury.

The DESC script

DESCRIBE: put into words the behaviour that is affecting you. Be clear and use any evidence that will support your argument.

EMOTION: disclose how you feel, whether irritated, angry, enraged or unhappy.

SOLUTIONS: discuss what can be done or you would like to be done to improve the situation.

CONSEQUENCES: Say what positive things might happen if changes are made and what might result if the behaviour is not improved.

People might never have been given feedback about their behaviour and you may be the first to do so. Bullies and those who use aggressive behaviour can get away with it for a long time. I have worked with some very difficult and challenging people. I have learned they do not plan to be obstructive. They do not waken each day and wonder who they can mess up or shout at. As often as not they have no idea how they come across and certainly no idea of how much power they wield. If only they knew it, just a whisper from them and most would rush to their bidding. They really do need the feedback.

The essentials of the DESC script are:

DESCRIBE

You must describe your difficult person's behaviour to him or her, precisely, face to face. A client was referred recently with the words 'This man needs a personality transplant'. Now how helpful is that? It certainly did not enable this person to change nor did it provide any concrete objectives. If you have any evidence of bad or inappropriate behaviour now is the time to produce it. Time sheets, if they have been late, reports of aggressive incidents – any feedback that that moves your discussion on from hearsay and gossip. Remember, these people are very good at defending themselves and maintaining the status quo, so collect your ammunition well in advance.

EMOTION

You must remember to talk about how **you** feel. This is such powerful feedback, especially if you have been trying to effect change for a while. You may feel that it puts you in a vulnerable position to do so but, believe me, it does not. The majority of people do not wish to cause mayhem and upset so this leverage can inspire change. A young woman on a training course talked about her sister who infuriated her. She would weekend in her flat, have wild parties to which she was never invited, and then leave the detritus for her to clear up. In the past she would swing from silent martyrdom to having screaming arguments. This time she used the DESC script and talked about how her sister's behaviour made her feel: left out, exhausted and put upon, with an overwhelming desire never to invite her again. The sister was nonplussed, to say the least. She had thought her sister hated her friends and so had never thought to include her. They had never helped with the cleaning because it was always completed by the time they surfaced the next day. Solutions were negotiated and certainly at the last contact, there had been a lasting peace.

SOLUTIONS

If it is a work situation, you may want your member of staff to write down their negotiated solutions. A lot of the compliance work carried out with GPs would suggest that if they asked us to write down how to take our medication, there would be fewer half empty bottles on shelves and less persistent infection around. However, we can make use of this research and have paper and pen handy.

CONSEQUENCES

Many people have little idea about the consequences of their behaviour. Perhaps they were just given things as children, instead of earning them, or charmed their way constantly out of scrapes. You may be the first person to talk about what will happen to them if they continue to behave in the same way. It would be very positive to point out the good consequences that would follow should their behaviour change in the desired direction.

The last essential is to provide a timescale for improvement and to monitor progress. If the seasoned difficult person knows that nothing will be followed up then there will be no motivation to change. It goes without saying that even the most minuscule movement in the right direction should be rewarded. If no one notices, why bother! If the right changes are not forthcoming, then keep on targeting the individual till they do.

The power of the DESC script lies in its directness. It is sharp, focused and you can remain relaxed as you communicate clearly how you feel. Why should your life be shortened by someone else's stupid behaviour?

Returning to directness for a moment, so many people have mentioned over the years how they are going to give a certain member of staff a 'flea in their ear' or 'a piece of their mind' or some such colourful threat. The reality is that when you meet that employee afterwards and ask how the interview went, they tell you that they discussed holidays and football but the manager talked vaguely about the work bit. In other words, giving bad news is never easy and we often try to sugar-coat it. This process so dilutes the interaction that the core message is lost. We may think we have had the conversation; the recipient has no clue about it. DESC allows you to be direct and stick to the point, no matter what. And it allows you to prepare in advance.

When someone is angry with you, it so easy to become defensive and fight fire with fire. In this process we lose sight of our purpose which is usually to get the other person to listen to us. If we want to be truly effective, instead of just winning the point, then we must find a way of admitting what is correct in our protagonist's argument. Have you ever tried arguing with someone who is agreeing with you? You just can't for any sustained period. Bob Sharpe, the psychologist who first introduced this concept to me, asked participants on his courses to role play extreme anger with him. It was a cathartic moment. You are not often given carte blanche to be as nasty as you like, but people on that course managed very well. Then he cleverly started to agree with them, not with everything, but selectively. They tried in vain to summon the previous aggressive stance. They just could not do it.

One word of caution though. You must be genuine in your agreement as adversaries smell artifice at a hundred yards. That is why you must be selective. No need to agree with any personal abuse that is hurled at you.

Let us not forget the purpose of calming the other person down. It is to resolve the conflict. So just like the DESC script, get to solutions quickly. What would they like you to do to fix the problem?

Steps to confidence at work

- Use the DESC script to handle the difficult colleague.

- Plan your interaction in advance, using DESC.

- When someone is angry with you, admit to any errors immediately, listen, and get to solutions quickly.

- Feel confident that you can deal with any difficult person anywhere.

Chapter Fifteen
Perseverance and enthusiasm

Perseverance

From the annals of history we know that persistence and perseverance are keys to success, Edison and the light bulb come to mind, but in our own lives we give up too easily. Apparently it takes at least seven points of contact with a client, be that e-mail, letter, phone call, meeting, to get one piece of business. I can't count how many clients give up on their sales process long before that.

So persistence works. You may have to try different ways to reach your clients or different products to inspire them to buy, but keeping going is what it is all about.

Perseverance works at the personal level too.

How often do we think of wildly persuasive arguments on the way home after a difficult encounter? If we had only thought of them when faced with our personal nemesis. These days are over when you use the five strategies rule for the ninth influencing principle, perseverance.

If you need to influence a boss about promotion, new equipment, time off, whatever you might want, the secret is to construct five strategies to influence. If you put just a single argument forward then it can be easily dismissed by a leader who is not particularly motivated to help you.

There are a few key ingredients to the five strategies rule.

- Plan your strategies in advance.
- All strategies should take into consideration what is in it for the other person to give you what you want.
- Five separate strategies are more difficult to dismiss. One is easy.
- Choose a time to influence when you have undivided attention.
- Prepare any research beforehand and take spreadsheets or financial projections with you. Have your evidence ready.

Let me give you an example.

CASE STUDY

My PA, Angie, wanted to go on a Sage accountancy course. She took me out to lunch and started by saying that it would be good personal development if she went on this course. Since I lived and breathed personal development this would be in line with my beliefs. Going on to argue that it would not take long, she said that she would use some of her holiday to train and so would only be out of the office for a minimum amount of time. She then presented me with the dates and hours involved. Finally she produced a spreadsheet with the return on investment for her course with a cost benefit analysis. Wow! She had already persuaded me at the first argument for personal development but I was enjoying the production. How marvellous; she had read and tried the five strategies rule. As a boss, it was interesting to experience as she combated any argument I might have had in advance. She had done her homework and that is always impressive. While I am writing this book she is on her course.

Dr Raj Persaud came up with a wonderful aphorism. It is that 'you have only two options in life; you can problem-solve or emotionally cope'. He announced this to a group of psychologists at a conference in Glasgow. They tried every argument to find a way round this adage and failed. Struggling, someone finally said, 'Well, if you can't problem-solve or emotionally cope then you would just have to die'. Dr Persaud replied that this would cover both options at once; problem-solving and emotionally coping.

In essence, I think the Raj recommendation was too simple for the psychologists present, who like nothing better than a complex theory. Of course there are a million ways of problem-solving and equally as many of emotionally coping but it is the simplicity of decision making that is compelling. Can I solve this or do I have to back off, let go, and cope with the result? The first option of problem-solving requires persistence, coming up with ideas and ways and arguments to get where you want to be.

Our scammers were a persevering lot, staying in their targets' houses for up to five hours running arguments, bargains, discounts, visions of health and well-being past these poor people. I think in the end they got orders because folk just wanted them out of their homes. Of course, cleverly, these salespeople were on another's turf so their customers couldn't leave. They came from a generation that were too polite to show them the door. This was all cleverly calculated. Nightmarish!

For our good endeavours, perseverance works too. A rule of thumb might be, if you are ready to give up try again just one more time.

Enthusiasm

Enthusiasm is a major influencer because it has a contagious effect. We want it for ourselves, as it lifts our spirits. And, of course, if you can't be enthusiastic for who you are or what you have you can't expect anyone else to be.

I was training a group of senior executives recently in media skills. In their midst was an experienced leader who had a very 'deadpan' sense of humour. He was funny but never smiled. His style simply did not work on television as he came across as downbeat, negative and serious which he clearly was not. So there is something around energy and openness that is important to engage and therefore influence.

In fact outright fun is persuasive. In Daniel Goleman's book *Emotional Intelligence*, two groups were given the same challenging task to perform. One group viewed a documentary before completing its task, the second group watched an episode of *Fawlty Towers*. Guess which group completed their task more competently? The *Fawlty Towers* group of course. There is a stack of evidence that when we laugh and have fun we learn more easily and simply perform better.

During the last American election I was asked by the BBC to comment on video footage to predict the outcome. Sarah Palin, whatever we make of her strange views, was funny with her 'lipstick on a pig' joke. And what an influence that had. Politics has such a dearth of fun attached to it that anyone who lightens the load will stand out. Of course world poverty and the financial crisis are serious stuff but it is poor influencing to be so depressing your audience become suicidal. In the 2006 movie 'Man of the Year' Robin Williams becomes President of the United States by mistake. He was a stand-up comedian who ran for president and a computer program malfunction erroneously elected him. He was so funny everyone loved him and he was inspirational. I know it is a movie and not real life, but it made me aware of the absence of fun in public life.

Often when you see ex-politicians interviewed they appear to have become witty observers. Perhaps they had always been funny but thought levity a vote loser. *Au contraire*, I am sure fun at the hustings would increase credibility and cheer us all up.

Comic Relief, with its Red Nose Day is held up as the most influential and successful charity of all time. Their message of fun while doing good is a powerful influencer. The fun part is a What is in it for me (WIIFM), the doing 'good' a What is in it for them (WIIFT). A true WIN-WIN.

Going back to our unprincipled influencers, they were certainly enthusiastic about their products even though the people they were selling to clearly were not. Quite the reverse in fact. So these influencing skills must be put to better use.

Steps to confidence at work

- Outline five strategies for influencing in advance of any negotiation with a boss or colleague. One strategy can be dismissed, whereas five shows persistence.

- It takes seven points of contact to acquire new business from a client.

- You have two options in life. Problem-solving or emotionally coping. Work out which to pursue.

- If you are about to give up, try one more time.

- Enthusiasm and fun are compelling influencers of other people.

Chapter Sixteen
Confident networking

We carried out an audit recently in RTG and discovered that the majority, 89 per cent, of projects were due to meeting people, liking them, talking about what we do and ultimately doing business. Networking had supplied the majority of our business. This was a huge surprise to us.

Clients often ask me about the secrets of networking. Are they doing it already; should they be doing more; is there some talisman that will ensure success? The ten principles of influencing that we have discussed underlie the skills of good networking. Understanding and practising these will turn you into a confident networker.

I have to say I really dislike those network organizations where you talk for a minute about what you do and expect people to refer you to their clients. They are usually the wrong people with the wrong kinds of clients. The whole thing is designed to make you feel the pressure of commitment; commitment to give to your friends and colleagues these people that you would never do business with yourself. Networking hell!

A client of mine went to something even worse. Speed networking where you spend five minutes selling your wares before you move on to another eager soul. She felt there was something wrong with her because she did not immediately go 'whoop-de-doop, what a wonderful idea'. I reassured her that finding this kind of thing anathema was a sign of discernment and good taste.

Since we are talking about what networking isn't, let's get the negatives out on the table before we proceed with what I think it is.

What networking is not

It is not about selling; yourself or your business. You can see the glint of desperation in the eye of the consultant and it is often consultants who man or woman these networking clubs. You just know you are going to be sold something you don't want to buy. You see them working the room with their target of meeting a certain number of people because they were told it was a numbers game. Business cards traded like casino chips, the organized ones returning home to tick boxes on their spreadsheet of conquests.

What networking is

Networking is about forming relationships first and foremost. It is about relating to the people you meet and like with no ulterior motive except to exchange ideas, perhaps information, to share similar interests and suggest meetings with others. It is helping others get what they want.

I am not so cynical as not to believe that the reciprocity of these relationships might of course lead to business, but it is not the goal of interaction. To network you must like the people you are interacting with or it does not work. It also helps if where you meet them has a purpose above and beyond networking; a charity fund-raiser, an arts society, a political rally, a school reunion, a conference – somewhere where there are folk who share your interests.

To help you with your networking plans make a list of all the strands of your life where you could be meeting other like-minded individuals. Below is a list to trigger some specific thoughts of your own. You may be networking in some of these areas but there may also be gaps. Select those that most appeal and to which you can make a genuine contribution.

Networking list

- school friends and former pupils
- university alumni networks
- specialist, or professional bodies
- work-based forums for discussion
- interest groups, political and community
- charity events and fund-raising groups
- hobbies and sports groups
- religious communities
- arts organisations
- boards and committees on which you might want to serve
- neighbourhood networks and friendships

Steps to confidence at work

- Networking is about forming relationships with like-minded people and helping them get what they want.
- Enhance and broaden your network.
- Be generous with your support.
- Use the ten principles of influencing for networking.

Part Four
Be a confident leader

Chapter Seventeen
Be aspirational

If you are working in an office aim to be the manager. If you are a manager train to be a director. If a director, raise your sights to the position of MD. Be aspirational.

A few years ago I was commissioned to travel round schools, helping young women in the fifth and sixth years raise their sights toward more senior positions. It was interesting to note how many had low expectations of their abilities and therefore of their career advancement. With the skills of self-esteem and confidence they flourished. As years have gone by we know that interventions such as this have worked and it is young men who now require support.

Confidence is unequivocally at the heart of everything at work and leadership is no exception. I would go as far as to say that without confidence you will be a very poor leader indeed.

When I first started as an entrepreneur, hiring my own team, I would pooh-pooh any idea of being the 'boss'. I stood for egalitarianism and felt that the position of Big Cheese was outmoded and authoritarian. I was everyone's friend and they mine. I was part of the team. Now, many years later, I realize there is nothing wrong with being friendly with people at work as long as you are prepared to give feedback when folk screw up. The main thing, the deal breaker, is that you have to lead from the front.

I had to tell myself 'It is your company. You set the values and style of interaction. You are the leader.' I realized I was shying away from the term not because of the philosophical niceties of equal opportunity, but through low self-esteem; to be the leader sounded swanky and above myself. I had to give myself a pep talk.

Leadership is important but you have no idea just how important!

In an article in the *British Psychological Society Magazine* in September 2009, the author Jacob Hirsh revealed that a CEO influences the profitability of a company by 15 per cent. Plus 15 per cent if they are a good leader, minus 15 per cent if a poor one. That's a whopping 30 per cent differential. The two major factors of significance were PERSONALITY and cognitive ability – THINKING.

Personality

Of the five Goldberg Personality Factors – extraversion, agreeableness, conscientiousness, emotional stability and openness – conscientiousness and emotional stability were the two that made the most difference to performance outcome. In other words, to the bottom line.

Cognitive ability

This comprises intelligence but also thinking, decision making and problem solving.

This predicted effect of a leader on a team, department or company had the highest correlation ever in psychological research ($r = .65$ for those statisticians amongst you). Just to give you some perspective, the result was four times more predictive than Ibuprofen on a headache and twice that of Viagra on other parts of the body. So leadership is important.

CASE STUDY

Eric invested in a company offering HR consultancy to small and medium sized businesses. The MD suddenly decided he was retiring and virtually disappeared the next day. Eric was left with a company that he liked as an investment but certainly not to run. He knew nothing about HR. He was a financier for goodness sake. There were scattered offices throughout the UK so he began travelling most weeks to try to understand the business and to keep control of activity.

The women, all the employees in the firm were female, mourned the loss of the previous incumbent and so when Eric asked them to do something differently, or anything at all really, he was ignored. The business began to lose money; it was a rudderless ship. What was Eric to do? He was a nice man who did not make decisions quickly but nettles were not being grasped. He was not leading from the front.

One of our coaches revealed to him that he was indecisive and had a fear of taking control. This feedback was sufficient to enable a personal and business reappraisal. He kept the staff in the London office, where he worked, and offered a financial package to the scattered outposts either for relocation or support to leave. The majority chose to leave. He has now recruited the team he wants and is making progress in the marketplace. Sometimes you just have to take the lead and make the tough decisions for the sake of the business.

Here are the ingredients of good leadership so that you can add 15 per cent to your bottom line.

In terms of personality

Be conscientious

- Have a vision for future success.
- Provide mission statements every six months to deliver to deadlines.

Be cool

- Learn to relax and sleep.
- Institute a work–life audit every few months.
- Understand your power as a leader.

In terms of thinking

- Have ideas and problem solve.

The following chapters will deal with each of the six skills outlined above for confident leadership to enable you to lead from the front.

Steps to confidence at work

- Go for posts that offer promotion.
- Be prepared to lead from the front.
- As a leader of a team, department or company you can make a serious difference to the bottom line of your organization.

Chapter Eighteen
Be conscientious

For a leader to be conscientious it is not enough to work hard. There are others in your employ to consider and they must move towards the same goal as you and deliver what you want. This next section discusses the skills to help you become a conscientious and therefore confident leader.

1. Vision

'Leadership is an ability to paint the picture of what success looks like and articulate it.'

Peter Lederer
Chairman of Gleneagles Hotels

Many leaders think that the company vision for the future is up for grabs and all can join in. This is mistaken. It is the leader's job to create the vision and mission statements. You can always tell a vision statement created by committee. For a start they are never concise statements more like treatises as they try to keep everyone happy. You will see them in reception areas with numerous bullet points. No one looks and no one remembers. What a well-intentioned waste of time.

Look at the Bimbo and Boeing visions. They have 'group think' written all over them. Boeing's first statement is fine, if a bit woolly. The rest is lovely but who could remember it. Compare it with an old Starbucks one; '2000 coffee shops by the year 2000'. Now call me old-fashioned but I would remember that. In fact, as I was writing this section my computer crashed and I lost all the vision material I had collected. It was interesting to note the ones I remembered. They were the clever, the short, and the punchy.

Bimbo

We are:

- The world leader in the baking industry and one of the best companies in the international food industry.
- A company with trustworthy, leading brands for our consumers.
- Our customers' preferred supplier.
- A strong and sound company for our stakeholders.
- A forward-looking company.
- An extraordinary place to work in.

Boeing

People working together as a global enterprise for aerospace leadership.

- People – A company, any company, is nothing more or less than the people who make it up.
- Working – This is about effort. Work. We all have a task to do. We are here to provide value to our shareholders, to Boeing people, and to communities where we work.
- Together – Every organization has forces that try to divide and reduce the impact of the total. Lockheed Martin does. Airbus does. And Boeing does. The more we can pull together, share knowledge, the stronger we will be.
- One – We have a shared destiny. We will succeed or fail together. There is one Boeing stock price. This is a powerful concept. It can make us more efficient and competitive. For example, having a leak in a boat and not helping each other bail out the water is not a successful strategy. Looking for common solutions to problems, sharing facilities, sharing services, are all part of being 'One.'

- Global – If we are to compete effectively in the next century, we will be a global company. Our team will reflect global backgrounds and global experience.

- Company – A company is a cohesive, inclusive institution. The dictionary uses words like 'assemblage', 'fellowship.'

- Aerospace – We are an aerospace company. We are not going to build railcars or boats. We are going to build aerospace products: airplanes, launch vehicles, satellites.

- Leadership – We are not here to be also-rans. We are here to lead, to be the best, nothing less.

During an interview with me, Brian Davis, former CEO of the Nationwide Building Society, talked about the importance of short vision and mission statements. When you have three people, even thirty people, a company can still be about you but, he said, when you have three hundred or three thousand it has to be all about them. And to mobilize that number of people you require a good memorable vision for the future.

Actually I think even with three it should be all about them if you want their help to build your business.

You are about to prepare your own vision of the future. Imagine where you want to be in the marketplace, with what product, with whom. A vision should last for two to three years, perhaps longer if it is a good call to action, and then it will need to be updated. Start to write down any ideas that come to you. Here are some guidelines.

Guidelines for a memorable vision statement

One sentence – any longer and you forget.

Specific to your company and marketplace – give me a pound for every vision that is 'be the best that you can be'. Ho hum! Your vision should make business sense and be unique to your organization.

Motivational – a vision should propel and inspire you and others towards a future goal.

Stretching – it should move everyone on to higher achievements beyond the everyday.

Moral – some feeling of good for all is compelling.

Aesthetically pleasing – your use of language should be crafted to look and sound good. It has to last for some years.

Action oriented – 'a vision without action is a daydream, action without vision is a nightmare', an old Japanese proverb.

Vision examples

Have a look at the examples below and choose your favourites, then craft your own in their likeness.

Amazon.com
Our vision is to be earth's most customer centric company; to build a place where people can come to find and discover anything they might want to buy online.

Dell
Dell listens to customers and delivers innovative technology and services they trust and value.

eBay
eBay pioneers communities built on commerce, sustained by trust, and inspired by opportunity.

Google
To organize the world's information and make it universally accessible and useful.

Starbucks
Starbuck's vision was 2,000 shops by the year 2000.

Microsoft
Bill Gates' Microsoft vision was – There will be a personal computer on every desk running Microsoft software.

Chrysler
Lee Iacocca's vision statement when at Chrysler was: If you find a better car.... buy it!

Kraft
Kraft's vision is helping people round the world eat and live
  better.

Nike
Nike in the 1990s Crush Adidas.

Johnson and Johnson
Put the needs and wellbeing of the people we serve first.

Henry Ford
About the automobile; when I'm through.....everyone will have
  one.

So now create your vision for your team, department, company, or
just yourself.

Create your overall vision for your business or part of a business
below.

Your vision

Mission statements to deliver to deadlines

Brian Davis, my guru for all things visionary, told me that he would
retire to a hot bath to contemplate the goals for the ensuing six
months and come up with a slogan to focus the troops. These he
called mission statements.

So now that you have articulated your vision, think of what you and your colleagues are going to focus on over the next six months to get to your overall vision. Your slogan should not be more than six or seven words as that is all we remember easily. So start with a list of all that you need to achieve. Notice if any themes emerge and bring those together in a sentence. Focus on keywords and cut out extraneous pronouns and verbs.

Now you have a punchy slogan.

Guidelines for a mission statement

Positive – think inspirational.

Short and pithy – think TV ad.

Commercial – think business difference.

In the boxes below write:

Your business mission statement

Your personal mission statement for the role you plan to play in your business

> 1. Team/company/department mission statement

> 2. Your personal mission statement

With your team slogan in place come up with some ideas of where you can emblazon it for the next six months. Mugs, tee shirts, banners round the office, screen savers, anywhere that reminds everyone of the focus of endeavours. With so many distractions, missions are forgotten and tangents followed. Be creative with your mission merchandise.

Steps to confidence at work

- Articulate a vision of what you want to happen at work and talk about it often. It takes people with you.
- Create a slogan for a motivational mission statement every six months. Create one for yourself too as it keeps you on track.

Chapter Nineteen
Be cool

Emotional stability is of paramount importance for a confident leader as it creates consistency and calm. Someone who is jolly one day and aggressive the next is so unpredictable that no one ever knows where they are with them. That is no good for the confidence of those around them.

I worked as a consultant for just such a leader. Every day as she arrived at the office, I noticed staff peering into reception trying to see what mood she was in; a frown denoted a bad mood and people scattered, a smile and they hovered. What time was wasted and stress engendered.

In transactional terms such a leader will be critical parent one day, perhaps feel bad about their behaviour, then be fun-loving child the next. They constantly swing between the two, never confronting their issues rationally in adult mode.

This section looks in detail at three strategies to enable emotional stability to flourish and therefore increase your confidence.

Relaxation

Daniel Goleman, when I asked him what he first noticed about people, said it was how relaxed or not they were. 'If someone is uptight it is a signal that something is off.'

Things do go off when we are stressed. We eat speedily and badly, sleep intermittently, exercise less and become snappier with people.

I had always seen myself as a benevolent and empowering boss, interested in all of my team. But when I went through a 360° assessment,

I received feedback that this view of me was not always how I was perceived. Apparently, when I returned from travelling and working abroad they noticed I had little time for them and when they spoke to me I looked out of the window. To say the least, I was nonplussed. On contemplation, I realized that travelling was tiring and the additional stress of returning to an overflowing desk meant that I was focused on tasks, not people. I really was tempted to say 'I am doing all this hard work to pay your wages'. But in that moment I realized that was not the point. They wanted me there and interested in them. Above all they required me to be relaxed. I made sure that I booked one-to-one meetings, especially after a long trip.

We are honed to perfection for short-term stress, the kind generated by going for an interview, making that all important presentation, getting out of a burning building. Long-term stress is a different matter.

Hans Selye, the French Canadian researcher, stated that it takes about three weeks to habituate to a stressful lifestyle of the sort I described above. The danger is that you are unaware of your high stress levels. And there are plenty of jobs around which require the commitment of working long hours and taking work home. Or at least people think that is what they have to do to keep up. So three weeks of constantly working late and you have tipped over into long-term stress and you won't even know it.

Today's humans still have the same nervous system as their prehistoric ancestors. Catch or be caught was the rule of the jungle. Life today is less absolute with many people subjecting themselves to the stress of the wrong job, being bullied by a superior or being married to the wrong person. This long-term stuff lowers self-esteem and limits our ability to tackle the issues.

Take a look at the stress signature checklist and see if any of the physical, psychological or behavioural signs are in evidence in your life.

FIGURE 19.1   Your stress signature

Your stress signature	Often	Occasionally	Never
Physical Signs			
Chest Pain			
Diarrhoea			
Headache			
Indigestion			
Sleep Problems			
Palpitations			
Tiredness			
Allergies			
Colds			
Psychological Signs			
Negative thinking			
Inability to relax			
Irritability			
Poor memory			
Reduced concentration			
Intolerance for eg noise			
Mood swings			
Sexual problems			
Behavioural Signs			
Awkward positions of body			
Poor posture			
Fidgeting			
Pacing up and down			
Restless			
Always rushed			
Drinking too much			
Disorganization			

The more scores you have in the 'often' and 'occasionally' categories the more you are showing signs of stress. It is also worth looking at the pattern of the scores. Are they all in one section or spread over two or three? It is important to note where they occur so that you recognize the pattern of your particular signs and symptoms.

When we become stressed, it would appear that we adopt a whole plethora of unhelpful responses. We know that we should relax, take exercise, eat vitamin-rich food, but do we do it? Apparently not.

> The relaxation formula
>
> Power minute
> Five-minute break
> Fifteen-minute lunch
> Sleep soundly

The power minute

We all breathe and yet, believe it or not, the majority of us do it badly. Give yourself the one minute breathing test. Discover the number of breaths you take in a minute (in and out counts as one).

Between 10 and 12 is an average number of breaths. More than that and you are breathing too rapidly and your breaths are too shallow. It is not so much that you are not taking in enough oxygen, but that you are not breathing out sufficient carbon dioxide.

When tense, our breathing tends to speed up automatically. By slowing it down you also decrease your heart rate and pulse rate. Breathing out is the important part of the process as it rids the lungs of stale air, stops us feeling dizzy and muscles are less cramped and sore.

The more relaxed we are, the more effectively we work. Stress on the other hand makes us worried about ourselves and distracts us from those around us.

Try the one minute breathing test again, this time breathing in and out more slowly while allowing yourself to slow down.

This relaxed breathing is the power minute and it will energize you while focusing you on the business at hand. It is only a minute, so even the most stressed of you can make time for that. If you are working late then the power minute will help to identify priorities and increase concentration so that the time spent at your desk is halved.

Try the one minute breathing test and use the power minute on a regular basis. Of course, relaxation is about much more than this. To pursue it further, join a meditation or relaxation class, or purchase a CD. It takes three weeks to learn how to relax when you practise every day.

Advantages of relaxation

- Better concentration and memory.
- Increased creativity.
- Faster problem solving.
- Deeper sleep.
- Calm attitude to people issues.
- More effective immune system.

Five-minute break

Unions fought hard to get break pauses for employees during the working day but what happens now is that a tea or coffee break away from your desk is frowned upon in some companies. It may not be written down in tablets of stone but people just get the feeling that it is career limiting to do it.

Of course this is foolishness. Human beings have an average concentration span of about 1½ to 2 hours. This can be stretched if there is a crisis or a deadline to be met. But you cannot keep expecting to work continuously in that crisis mode. If you do not take a pause, your brain takes little 'micro sleeps'. That means you will catch yourself looking out of the window and then wondering where you were in that document, or even worse, when driving, how you got there. If you do not take a break your brain will do it for you. Of course your productivity is reduced if you are in micro sleep mode. Much better is to take that five minute break to return to your desk refreshed and focused.

Fifteen-minute lunch

Taking a fifteen-minute lunch is similar in philosophy to the five-minute break. The main thing is that your lunch does not have to take an hour as that may be too long to be away from your desk. But you still need a break. Getting out for a walk or even just eating your lunch on the other side of your desk manages to break concentration and revitalize you.

Sleep

I asked my group of 20 eminent leaders and opinion formers about the circumstances when they lacked confidence, the majority cited tiredness as the cause.

If you are working hard, you do not want to be burdened with insomnia. And yet that is when it is most likely to happen. There are tips for getting a good night's sleep below. Mark any that you think might be useful to you.

Insomniacs often develop strange habits at bedtime when they don't sleep. They surround themselves with books, magazines, music, TV and videos, going to bed early just in case sleep might catch them unawares. For a sleeping pattern to be established, a bed must be associated with relaxation not stimulation.

A work–life audit

It is so easy to become a 'one dimensional' creature who only works, sleeps and works again. This is not what successful and confident leaders do. Making time for other pursuits is not only stimulating but also relaxes as you focus on something completely different.

Using the work–life audit grid below write down:

- the positives of spending more time at work;
- the complaints you might get if you spend more time or focus too much on work;
- the positives of spending more time at home;
- the complaints you might get if you focus too much on your home life.

Work–Life Audit Grid

FIGURE 19.2 Work–life audit

Work	
Positives	**Complaints**
Home	
Positives	**Complaints**

So to get back to the audit, we might think that if we spend more time at work then home life will just have to suffer and vice versa. The big question here is what actions can you take to be in the positive quadrants for both work and home?

Understanding your power

A major contributor to a lack of confidence comes from not knowing how to manage the power of your position. Many roles contain an innate power base as colleagues' or employees' livelihoods are dependent on your good graces. The elegance with which you handle this power is the essence of good, confident leadership.

CASE STUDY

A manager in an electronics firm who was working with one of our coaches had just been promoted to director of a region. This was a global business, so he had a large number of employees to lead. He had been in post for six months but he knew none of his staff. It was only flagged up when he complained to the coach that no one came by his office to talk to him or had even tried to befriend him. The coach asked what made him think it was their job to get to know him. Should he not be the one to introduce himself and explore who he had in his employ? Apparently he didn't want to inflict himself on the staff as 'the big boss' so he stayed in his room. The staff thought he was stand-offish and had already decided he was a poor leader. Shying away from the power of the position is not the answer.

Write down below some examples of good and bad power then we can discuss how you use power at the moment. You might want to name names or simply highlight attributes.

Think back to personal experiences when you have felt the results of power. What effect did it have and did it help or hinder you? Focus on your parents too, and remember how you reacted to their use of power over you. The way you reacted to them is probably the way you react to authority figures now.

The obvious contenders for bad power must be the Hitlers of this world. In a business context, bad power is much more likely to be used for undermining, humiliating and manipulating people. Sometimes very bright leaders are unaware that they make others feel stupid as they highlight errors in open forum. Universities especially harbour those tendencies but there are also other businesses and institutions that are full of critical feedback they call intellectual rigour. They may substantiate such behaviour as keeping up standards and may even posit that such excoriating criticism is about the work and not the person. But, of course, people are attached to their work and it would be foolish to believe otherwise.

FIGURE 19.3 Examples of good and bad power

examples of power	
good power	**bad power**

I am not for a moment saying that there should be no criticism but I am emphasizing that this is not the best way to encourage. Remember the 8 to 1 rule we talked about in the influencing section of Part Three. So bad power can be used to undermine others and establish superiority, saying 'I'm OK but you are not'.

CASE STUDY

James was founder and MD of a small but very successful software company. He was 'a big brain' who used his cleverness to humiliate others. Nothing was ever good enough for James. He would pick up a report and throw it down with a sneer saying 'call this a report?' He paid well but expected his pound of flesh. I had the job of telling him that his staff feared him and this was destructive to his business success. He was heading towards the minus 15 per cent end of the leadership spectrum, as all his staff were on the point of resigning. That use of power just does not work.

If you are skimming this book go back and take a look at my favourite theories in Part One. How we transact with people reveals how we use power. As a psychologist and a coach, I realize how predictive the transactional analysis model of parent, adult, child behaviour is. If you are high critical parent you are more likely to use any power you have to undermine by fault finding. As nurturing parent you will kill with kindness rather than foster independence. A high natural child means power is used for jokiness and poking fun with no responsibility for the results; high adapted child either uses power to be manipulative, doing things behind backs, or abdicates power in a desire to be polite.

A good balanced use of leadership power is in evidence with the rational behaviour of the adult. Adult mode thinks things through, has a planned response to people, and, above all, is relaxed and emotionally stable. People in that mode will relinquish power if it helps to resolve a situation and always want a win-win when negotiating. They do not have to be top dog at all costs.

So a judicious use of power as a leader helps you get what you want, can influence for good, and establishes a culture of empowerment and fun. If you remember, in Chapter 2 Fraser Doherty of SuperJam used his power as a young entrepreneur to set up a charity that works alongside his business to help isolated older people by inviting them to afternoon teas. He is wildly successful. He told me quite sincerely that his interest is not in making loads of money (though he has). He wants to love what he does and make a difference. That seems like really good power and good leadership. He also comes across as very cool.

> Banish the word heresy if you want to be a good leader. Be prepared to be challenged from the bottom up.
>
> Ian McMillan
> Director of CBI Scotland

Steps to confidence at work

- Learn to relax with the power minute.

- Be aware of your stress signature, as it is your mind and body wanting you to make changes.

- Use a work–life audit frequently to test if you are over-focusing. You can get the best out of life and work. One does not have to be at the expense of the other.

- Be cool and use your power well.

Chapter Twenty
Be bold, have ideas

Confidence is having your own ideas, taking a view. And not just having ideas but confidence is also putting your head above the parapet and airing them.

CASE STUDY

A young woman called Veronica came to me for coaching as she wanted to become more confident. She looked fabulous, very much the thrusting young executive with designer briefcase. But she had nothing to say about the financial services product she was selling. Exploration of the problem revealed that she left the business development to her co-director while she remained in the background dealing with the running of the office. All would have been fine if she had been happy with that but she was not. Helping her to find her voice by coming up with ideas for the business that she, and only she, could deliver changed her working life. Her clearly defined role now is that she deals with all the businesswomen who approach the consultancy as she discovered that many women like to deal financially with another woman. She delivers the presentations and selects the financial product that is best for her female clients. Veronica came out of the shadows.

Confidence is not associated with being silent and compliant. If you know you can produce ideas, solve problems and come up with ways round a situation then you will be supremely confident.

Number one on the list of ten commandments for success gleaned from my interviews with 80 chief executives for the book *Fast Track to the Top* was problem-solving. Volunteering to solve things no one else wanted to touch got them noticed and propelled them to senior office. So clearly this is a major skill for confidence and success.

This chapter will look at your brand of creativity so that you are confident to contribute.

Confidence, creativity and you

Respond to each of the following questions.

1   What is your personal definition of creativity? How might you tell a ten-year-old about creativity?

2   When are you at your creative best?

3   How do you know that you have been creative?

4   When do you tell others that they have been creative?

5   What stops you from being more creative?

Creativity is often seen as a special, rare commodity, mostly the province of off-the-wall artistic types. Of course there are some people who do continually have unusual ideas that are ground-breaking but that is at the extreme end of the spectrum. In general, we are all creative and can make a contribution when it comes to ideas and problem-solving.

There are many definitions, but one might include the ability to take existing things and combine them in different ways for new purposes. For example, Gutenberg took the wine press and the die punch and produced a printing press. So a simple definition of creativity is the ability to generate novel and useful ideas and solutions to everyday problems and challenges.

I certainly never saw myself as creative and it was only when I went to the Creative Problem Solving Institute (CPSI) in the States and people opted to be in my team because they saw me as creative that I had to change that view of myself.

My contribution to creativity is that I experience techniques from another sector and can then adapt and tailor them for a different use, all with the aim of helping others in coaching and personal development.

People often answer question 2 by saying they are, for example, mostly creative when waking, in the shower or on holiday. Very rarely is the answer 'at work'. The problem with the average workplace is that it is too stressful with the pressures of deadlines and busy work to engender the calm necessary. Creativity requires relaxation to flourish. So the environment must be conducive to ideas being generated.

Questions 3 and 4 are challenging for many people. They don't always know they have been creative and if they don't know then they aren't into noticing when others are either. So the answer to this is that you have to be creative on purpose, not just when the mood takes you.

What comes out when discussing question 5 with participants on my courses is that there is no time at work to talk about ideas. Everyone is so busy dealing with the here and now that ideas for the future are forgotten or fall off the end of the agenda as other more pressing problems take precedence.

If you can remember back to Part 2, Branding for Confidence, you completed a leadership styles questionnaire and discovered if you were a diplomat, an organizer, a strategist or a tactician. These styles are all also associated with distinctive types of creativity. Work out what your approach to creativity is from the chart, Figure 20.1 below.

The discovery of your type of creativity is a confidence boost in itself as you realize you can contribute in your own distinctive way. You do not have to leave ideas about your work to others. You have a voice.

My PA, for example, is an organizer and likes nothing more than conjuring up a table or a spreadsheet so that we all know what we are doing. She is a streamliner, a sorter of our office chaos. Bob, a tactician, loves editing our manuscripts and workbooks as he cannot bear poor grammar and has the vocabulary of a Winston Churchill. At the same time, as marketing director, he has a true passion for how we display our wares on our website. A true tactician. One of our coaches, Marthinus, is a strategist who loves the creativity of planning the big picture and making things happen. I, on the other hand, as the diplomat, love the creativity of vision and how I can get everyone on board to reach it.

We are all creative; just in different ways.

FIGURE 20.1   Creativity and leadership style

Diplomat	Organizer
Creativity is self-expression. My creativity involves me as catalyst or facilitator toward my own and others' creativity and in supporting development.	Creativity is effective improvement. My creativity stabilizes chaotic conditions for greater efficiency, safety and security – one step at a time.
Strategist	**Tactician**
Creativity is vision. My creativity involves me in applying competent analysis and strategy to make things happen in line with my vision.	Creativity is variation and boundary breaking. My take on creativity is that I troubleshoot for action and impact, depending on what the situation requires.

Steps to confidence at work

- Step out of the shadows and have a view about what you do and how it might be done better.
- Work out when you are most creative and be creative on purpose.
- Tell others about your ideas.
- Understand your distinctive take on creativity.

Chapter Twenty-one
Be charismatic – the ultimate in confidence at work

FIGURE 21.1 What is charisma?

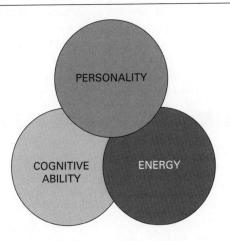

To complete Part Four, Be a confident leader, I felt it worth briefly exploring charisma and what it means when applied to leaders. We all have our favourite charismatic leaders. Let me tell you about one woman's brush with charisma.

CASE STUDY

Mary Wilson was head of administration in a global manufacturing company. She was in her forties, a single parent with a teenage son and a number of cats. She had travelled little in her life as she spent all her free time bringing up her son. Her boss was a delightful man, a very inclusive leader, and when he heard that his plant had won a training award to be received at the White House, he decided that his staff should make the trip to collect the award rather than the directors.

When I spoke to Mary before she left for her trip she was a little indifferent to the whole award thing but said that she was keen to go to the museums in Washington. The White House was not of much interest to her and she was disparaging about Clinton and his 'shenanigans' as she called his much publicized behaviour.

The next time I caught up with her was about a week after her return. She couldn't wait to talk to me. This otherwise grounded Scottish woman was positively girlish in her excitement. The difference was that she had met Bill Clinton. She was positioned in the front row and was in the best place to receive the full blast of his personality. She described his white shirt, his gaze around the room, his ability to make everyone feel special; his charisma.

She had been won over from indifference by the presence of the man.

So what is charisma? Do we leave the definition as some mystical quality or can we get a handle on it?

Richard Branson is often described as charismatic and yet he interviews poorly on television, he is hesitant and tense. What he does well though is be the action hero most men would love to be and most women find exciting. He has a different kind of charisma.

Leaders from various companies' high potential lists were interviewed, studied and assessed by their peer group in a recent research project. The results revealed that behavioural characteristics dependent on a person's energy levels, for example speed of movement, body language, eye contact and vocal projection, featured most highly in those considered to be exceptional.

Looking in more depth at energy-related personality qualities revealed enthusiasm, lack of social anxiety, openness, extraversion, agreeableness, a desire to be in charge and self-confidence. Yet those having these same personality traits but lacking in energy were considered less exceptional, less charismatic. This led to the conclusion that there was a component to charisma, separate from personality traits, which could be quantified, studied and developed. It was personal energy.

So here is the challenge, how can you generate and increase your personal energy, raising it to a charismatic level, and then communicate that quality in behaviour?

From my experience of leaders, energy comes from loving what you do, having a mission to get things done and therefore leading a meaningful existence.

Much has been written about charisma being insufficient for leadership success and that is in line with what we have been discussing in this part of *Confidence at Work*. Charisma is, of course, an attribute of personality, a major factor in Leadership success, but thinking and decision making are also key components.

For me, charisma is the sum of all the parts we have explored in this book.

It is about knowing who you are, being able to brand yourself for the outside world, having wonderful influencing skills, great problem solving abilities and leading from the front. These are the things that fuel the energy of charisma.

Ultimately we all have to live with ourselves, and what a shame if we look back on a life of missed opportunities and severed relationships. Confidence at Work allows you to look success in the face and decide to go for it – skilfully.

Steps to confidence at work

- Be energetic in your pursuit of success.
- Use each part of this book so that you can be considered charismatic.

Some final thoughts

The more you can bring the real you to work, express yourself through what you do and pursue your goals with energy and commitment, the more confident you will be. It is a wonderful thing about confidence that as soon as you embark on the journey you will notice the difference. If in addition, you start to call yourself confident then you will look for opportunities to show off your new skills. The whole process starts to escalate and expand.

As you become more confident at work, help others on their journey. People hide their lack of confidence, especially at work, so you do need to listen to those around you and pick up on the signs through what they say, how they say it and their body language. Become an expert at detecting a lack of confidence in others and then help them to overcome it with guidelines from this book.

Enjoy the journey towards Confidence at Work and I look forward to hearing about your successes.

Best wishes

Ros